Conversations

FACE TO FACE WITH YOUR LORD

Book 2

Conversations

FACE TO FACE WITH YOUR LORD

Book 2

Danika R. Salmans

Glory, Strength & Beauty
LARAMIE, WYOMING

Copyright © 2019 by Danika R. Salmans.

All rights reserved. No part of this publication may be reproduced, distributed or transmitted in any form or by any means, including photocopying, recording, or other electronic or mechanical methods, without the prior written permission of the publisher, except in the case of brief quotations embodied in critical reviews and certain other noncommercial uses permitted by copyright law. For permission requests, contact the publisher through the web site below.

All scripture quotations are from the King James Bible.

Danika R. Salmans/Glory, Strength, & Beauty Publishing
Laramie, Wyoming

www.GloryStrengthAndBeauty.com

Book Layout ©2015 BookDesignTemplates.com

Conversations/ Danika R. Salmans. —1st ed.

ISBN 978-0-9991209-2-7

Dedicated to Nathan.

I love you, I love you. You are my boy.
I love you, I love you, You are my boy.
You brighten my day from morning to night.
I love you, You are my boy.

And the LORD spake unto Moses face to face, as a man speaketh unto his friend.

Exodus 33:11

Contents

Preface xi
Acknowledgements xiii
Introduction 1
59: The Unredeemed 9
60: A Loving Leader 13
61: My Friend, My Reproach 17
62: I Promise 23
63: Safe in the Camp of the Lord 27
64: I Got to See it Happen 33
65: Boundaries and Walls 37
66: Rise and Shine 43
67: Bethesda 49
68: Wait 53
69: You Can be a Prophet 59
70: Help Me 63
71: Glory to God 69
72: Stay in the Fold 75
73: Being a Leader 81
74: Fishing for the Praise of Men 87
75: I Cannot Go Beyond 93
76: Strive 99
77: Zealous 104
78: Speak Up 109

79: Stay Close 115
80: Lovest Thou Me 121
81: Take Time for Change 127
82: Desire, Vengeance, and Envy 133
83: I'm Just Talking 139
84: Life Sentence 143
85: Memory 149
86: The Mom Speech 155
87: Decide Now 161
88: Night Torments 167
89: Doubt and Deception 173
90: Me First 179
91: Why is He Here? 185
92: Which Way? 191
93: It is Not God's Fault 197
94: Pure Religion 203
95: Be Kind 209
96: Be Doing 215
97: Overtaken 221
98: I Know! 227
99: I Have a Pattern 233
100: The Impossible is Possible 237
101: Shine as Lights 243
Connect with others on Social Media 267
The Conversation Continues... **Error! Bookmark not defined.**

Preface

The book you are holding represents something very real and personal; this collection represents the result of my conversations with God. I want to share so that you can experience something wonderful; your own face-to-face relationship with God.

One day I asked myself, "Is it really possible for the Lord Jesus to speak to me through my Bible?" I had been in a routine of reading my Bible every morning, but rarely did I come away with anything real and tangible. I never really felt that the Lord spoke to me through my reading. I desired to hear from Jesus, but I wondered if it was actually possible to receive a personal message on a regular basis from reading my Bible.

I decided that I was going to open my Bible with expectation. I was going to be attentive and watchful while reading. I continued with my normal routine of reading a passage from the Old Testament, New Testament, Psalms, and Proverbs for each day. That morning it was different from other mornings; I was watching and talking to the Lord as I read. I experienced something incredible that morning. As I read and talked with my Lord, I began to see a theme emerge. A common thread weaved those passages together. I knew the message was for me. I was amazed! I actually had a message from the Lord. Through His word, He revealed something I needed! I wrote the conversation down and thus, Conversation 1 was born.

The next day I sat down with my Bible and wondered, "Will it happen again. Will God speak and will I be able to hear it?" I read, watched and talked to my Lord. Sure enough, there it was again; a message from the Lord that was for me. I wrote my conversation down. Once again, the Lord had given me a personalized message from my open Bible; a message tailored for me and my life.

Each day I kept reading, watching, praying and writing. Sometimes the message that I received was painful. I had to recognize that the Lord was correcting me. This was not easy, but I had to keep the lines of communication open. I could not "hang-up" on Jesus because the discussion became difficult to bear. I had to keep my Bible open, watching and talking with the Lord.

My hope is that through this book, you will come to realize that you too can use your Bible to start a real conversation with the Lord. Sometimes the conversation will be difficult; many times it will be glorious and a sweet reminder of what He has done for you! Jesus is God, He is real, He is alive, and He can physically touch your life. He can relate to you in a genuine and tangible way through the pages of your Bible. He is not just something to believe in; He is someone you can talk to.

I pray that you will open the lines of conversation. Watch what happens as you open your Bible with expectation and talk with God. I would love to hear what your Lord has for you!

Danika Salmans

Acknowledgments

The completion of this book was not a solo endeavor. I was surrounded by many friends that prayed me through this effort. I could not have completed this book without their prayers for the Lord's direction.

I would like to express sincere appreciation and indebtedness to the following:

- Dana, for her encouragement and line-by-line review of the draft.
- Judy, for her review of the draft and lending perspective and advice.
- My husband, for applying his wisdom to ensure that this book is doctrinally sound.

Above all, I extend immense gratitude to my Lord and Saviour, Jesus Christ, for his guidance and direction. I look forward to what he has for me next.

Face to Face With Your Lord

Introduction

CONVERSATION. An exchange of ideas between two or more parties that involves both speaking and listening.

    For a conversation to begin, there are some requirements. You must have some sort of a defined relationship with the other person, you must have some mode of communication, and you must have a subject matter to discuss.

    Have you ever wanted to have a conversation with God? Exchanging thoughts and having a sweet moment to listen? Imagine walking side-by-side and just talking, listening, and learning. It would be purely divine! This is not beyond the realm of possibility. You can have an ongoing, face to face conversation with God. It takes a relationship with Jesus Christ, prayer as your mode of communication and the subject matter is what you have read in your Bible and how it applies to your life situations.

How can I connect with Jesus?

We have a connection problem with God.

> **1 Corinthians 2:14** But the natural man receiveth not the things of the Spirit of God: for they are foolishness unto him: neither can he know *them*, because they are spiritually discerned.

We need to have God's help in understanding His word and in discerning His hand in our lives; we need His nearness and we need to have a relationship with Him. But there is something that is blocking our connection with God. God is perfect and just, and the fact that we are "natural man" makes us much less than perfect. This difference in perfection forms a connection problem that we have no power to overcome.

How is this difference in perfection created? The Bible says that "... all have sinned, and come short of the glory of God;" (Romans 3:23) We define sin as wrongdoing or a transgression of God's law. Sin includes a failure to do what is right. It is violence and lovelessness toward other people, and ultimately, rebellion against God. Clearly, we have all sinned! In contrast, God does not sin as He is defined by love and His actions toward us are motivated by pureness and goodness. You can understand that there is a disconnect between man and God.

However, God loves you dearly, and He does not want your sin to prevent a relationship and a clear connection with Him. Everyone has the same problem. It is natural to do wrong, and the natural consequence of sin is separation from God. In this state, communication with God is severely limited.

So, how do you get rid of sin so you can have a connection with God? You can't "undo" your past sins. No amount of good deeds can erase past sin. In addition, we can't take our sins with us into heaven. Eternal separation from the God who loves you would now be your fate. What a horrible, helpless state we find ourselves in!

Now for the good news! Thankfully, God has solved this problem that separates us from Him; He has made a way to remove our sins so we can have a relationship with Him. God has given you a wonderful gift. God demonstrated His love for you when He became a "man" in the form of Jesus and provided payment for your sins when He died on the cross.

> **Romans 6:23** For the wages of sin *is* death; but the gift of God *is* eternal life through Jesus Christ our Lord.

<u>Jesus is God</u> and thus the only one who could pay for your sins in full. Jesus Christ lived a sinless life and died on the cross for your sin. He did not stay in the grave, as he rose again proving that He is God. When you accept His gift and let Jesus pay for your sins, He now owns them; you no longer own your sins, but instead, His righteousness.

> **2 Corinthians 5:21** For he hath made him *to be* sin for us, who knew no sin; that we might be made the righteousness of God in him.

With your sins forgiven and purchased by Jesus, you are now righteous (perfect) in God's eyes. You have a new nature and a revived spirit that can now connect with the Lord; sin is no longer breaking the lines of communication.

So, who has your sins? Do you still possess them, or have you let Jesus purchase them? If you still own your sins, you remain in your "natural" state. You cannot experience a close relationship with the Lord, and your spirit cannot hear His still small voice. Your sin separates you from a relationship here on earth and a home in heaven.

This does not have to be your fate. You can have a relationship with Jesus, and you can know your home will be heaven when you die. This is a decision you make or a gift you reject. If you want Jesus to pay for your sins, and you believe that His life, death, and resurrection proves He can pay, please pray and let God know you will accept His gift as payment for your sins.

> *"Lord, forgive me. I am a sinner. I am doomed to die separated from you because of all my sin. I now know that Jesus died to purchase my sins. I believe that he proved he was able when he rose from the grave. Lord Jesus, I want to make the trade. Please pay for my sins and I humbly take your righteousness. Thank you, Lord, for making a way for my sins to be cleared. This was not something that I could do for myself. Amen"*

This instantaneous transaction happens in your heart through faith. Once the trade has been made, you are cleared from your sin; your spirit can understand God's voice and the lines of communication are wide open. You can talk to God, and you have the means to hear from Him. Praise the Lord!

How do I pray?

Prayer is the mode of communication that you use to talk to your Lord. There are no particular words or fancy prayers that you must pray. In fact, Jesus said that he does not like repetitious words, he desires a real conversation.

> **Matthew 6:7** But when ye pray, use not vain repetitions, as the heathen *do*: for they think that they shall be heard for their much speaking.

Start talking to the Lord. Tell him anything that is on your heart. He loves to hear your voice. It is so sweet to speak to God! It is even sweeter when he speaks back!

Can God speak to me through my Bible?

Yes! Open your Bible and start reading with expectation. There will be parts that are difficult to understand so make that a part of your conversation with the Lord. In prayer, ask Him what it means. Ask Him what He wants you to get out of the passages.

Start a conversation with your Lord by opening your Bible and reading. God designed this book to speak to you. You can get something from the Bible that applies to your life today.

1 Timothy 4:13 Till I come, give attendance to reading, to exhortation, to doctrine.

Can the conversation be broken?

Yes! Once you have received Jesus' payment for your sin, the conversation can begin with a God that loves you. But there are things that you can do that will hinder the conversation. Unfortunately, your sin is still the element that will stifle communication with God. Even after receiving the gift of salvation, sin can still creep into your life and dull your ears to your Lord.

Psalms 66:18 If I regard iniquity in my heart, the Lord will not hear *me*:

To have ongoing conversations with God, you have to remove anything that would dull your ears to hearing from

God. The Bible tells you that God speaks in a still small voice and your heart condition will determine your ability to hear God's voice.

Some Christians can get to the point where they are incapable of hearing anything from the Lord because they have been unwilling to address sin in their life. The Bible promises you that if you will confess your sins (admit to the Lord that you did wrong) the Lord Jesus is faithful to forgive you of those sins and reestablish the lines of communication.

> **1 John 1:9** If we confess our sins, he is faithful and just to forgive us *our* sins, and to cleanse us from all unrighteousness.

Consistently confessing your wrongdoing to the Lord will ensure that the lines of communication will stay open. If you have accepted Jesus' payment for your sins, you CANNOT lose your status of being righteous in God's eyes. Jesus has ALL of your sins; past, present, and future. However, communication with God will be blocked if you have an unwillingness to admit your fault. If you have received the gift of salvation, but you are not living a life that honors God, then your sin will dull your ability to hear from your loving Lord.

Rejoin the conversation between you and Jesus Christ by confessing your sins and tune your ears to hear His sweet and gentle voice.

How to use this book?

The conversation begins with knowing that God is speaking to you and that you can hear what He has to say. Each conversation in this book is based on a set of passages from the Bible.

Conversations

Read the related Bible passages and then read the following conversation. After you have completed reading your Bible and reading the devotion, use the questions to guide your own conversation with the Lord. Enjoy your time with the Lord and talking with him throughout the day.

The conversation starts now...

Face to Face With Your Lord

CONVERSATION 59

The Unredeemed

Related Bible Passages			
Old Testament	Psalms	Proverbs	New Testament
Leviticus 24	53	30	Luke 21

I have seen Christians stunned by the behavior of those not yet redeemed. They cannot understand the unbeliever, and this can make them want to run, hide and cluster together with other Christians. The behavior of the unsaved might pull Christians to despise the lost to the point of never wanting to be near them. "Unclean, unclean!" they might scream to themselves and flee in order to keep their distance. In my conversation with the Lord, I was curious as to how we should approach this; what is the right balance? Should I remove myself and keep away from those that believe in a different way, or should I involve myself in their life so I can be an influence without being influenced?

As a Christian what am I to do? Am I to jump in their midst and risk "getting dirty" so that I can be a witness, or am I to keep my distance and live completely separate? After reading the passages above, I talked to the Lord about my disposition. How was I acting toward those that do not know the Lord?

Unbelievers will not act like a Christian, nor will they have the same motives as a Christian. It should not surprise us that they are acting out their unbridled flesh.

> **Proverbs 30:11-12** *There is* a generation *that* curseth their father, and doth not bless their mother. *There is* a generation *that are* pure in their own eyes, and *yet* is not washed from their filthiness.

But many Christians come to the conclusion that the best way to survive is to keep to themselves. Cluster together with those that are just like them for protection. Some follow the example of the law given to Moses and kick the sinners out of the camp!

> **Leviticus 24:23** And Moses spake to the children of Israel, that they should bring forth him that had cursed out of the camp, and stone him with stones. And the children of Israel did as the LORD commanded Moses.

Today, some people hold to the philosophy that wants to treat sinners the same way! Keep the heathen away! Stay out of our group; you do not belong! This is not the Lord's plan. In the New Testament, we can see time and time again the Lord Jesus having face to face interactions with unbelievers and making himself known to them. Christ's message is that we are to interact with sinners to help them kick sin out of their life. His message has never been for us to kick sinners out of our life.

The unsaved see the world in their own way. Most are serving themselves and are seeking personal happiness. They do not have the knowledge of a better way. The Spirit of the Lord does not reside within them to guide them and give them a new understanding and a new purpose for being on this earth. Those that believe that there is no God have their actions and decisions shaped by this viewpoint.

> **Psalm 53:1** The fool hath said in his heart, *There is* no God. Corrupt are they, and have done abominable iniquity: *there is* none that doeth good.

Their belief that there is no God could be because they have not been introduced. We should not just stand there from a distance appalled and amazed. We should get close enough to make introductions.

The Lord showed me that I am to be involved in the lives of the unsaved so that I will be able to point them to the Lord. But He also warned me to be careful:

> **Luke 21:34** And take heed to yourselves, lest at any time your hearts be overcharged with surfeiting, and drunkenness, and cares of this life, and *so* that day come upon you unawares.

I am to be present in their lives, but don't let myself get to the point where I enjoy their ways. My job is to be available to be used by the Holy Spirit to pull the unsaved beyond what they know and bring them to understand something new, something better, something wonderful -- a one-on-one relationship with God.

Face to Face With Your Lord

Have a Conversation with Your Lord Jesus

☙ Lord, do I try to flee from sinners? If I do, of what am I afraid?

_____
_____

☙ Lord, what do I do to introduce you to those that are not believers?

_____
_____

☙ Lord, in what ways can I be more involved with the unsaved and help them see you?

_____
_____

☙ Lord, I want to see others come to know you. Please help me to introduce someone to you.

*Pray...*_____
_____
...listen

CONVERSATION 60

A Loving Leader

| Related Bible Passages ||||
Old Testament	Psalms	Proverbs	New Testament
Leviticus 25	54	1	Luke 22

After reading the Bible passages, I had to wonder how do I treat those that are under my authority or under my care: my children, other women, employees? Do I rule over them with rigor?

Leviticus 25:43 Thou shalt not rule over him with rigour; but shalt fear thy God.

Rigor is severity or strictness, stringency, severity, toughness, harshness, rigidity, inflexibility, demanding, difficult, or extreme. Consider these words; would these words describe how you deal with your children or with others?

Ruling with rigor has more to do with our disposition and attitude toward those that we direct than it has to do with the number or severity of the tasks.

The Lord brought back some memories of times I ruled with rigor instead of ruling with love. These were memories I regretted but I know the Lord wanted to use them to help me not make the same mistake. Have you ruled with rigor?

We are commanded to train our children. We are to teach them to have high moral standards, to be kind and to love the Lord, but this is not accomplished through harsh words, inflexibility, or disappointed looks.

Consider the prayer of the oppressed, the victim of rigor

> **Psalm 54:3** For strangers are risen up against me, and oppressors seek after my soul: they have not set God before them. Selah.

When we rule over our family member with rigor, they could come to the conclusion that we are far from God and He is not a part of our life. If we are treating our family members with rigor in the hope of making them spiritual, we are actually accomplishing the exact opposite. They do not see the love of God in us, they do not see God in our actions, and they will not be drawn toward Him.

As we approach our family with rigor, we are filled with our own ways and selfish motivations and not filled with the love that Christ has shown us.

> **Proverbs 1:31** Therefore shall they eat of the fruit of their own way, and be filled with their own devices.

When we live with joy and approach our family with pleasant expectations, our spirit will experience joy; if we approach those in our family with harsh and demanding expectations, our spirit will likely be filled with frustration as we are denied the desired results.

As we deal with our family, we must show them that they are valuable to us. We must let them know that they are loved by us and by the Lord. This goes farther toward motivating them to turn toward "right" than does demeaning them and communicating our "grave disappointment" in who they are. Dealing with people with rigor rarely brings about positive results.

The Lord defined a leader in the following way:

> **Luke 22:26-27** But ye *shall* not *be* so: but he that is greatest among you, let him be as the younger; and he that is chief, as he that doth serve. For whether *is* greater, he that sitteth at meat, or he that serveth? *is* not he that sitteth at meat? but I am among you as he that serveth.

This was not an easy conversation for me to have with my Lord as I know I have been guilty of ruling my children with rigor. But as a leader, as a mom, I realized I do not need to rule with rigor and harsh words in order to accomplish godly results. My rigorous methodology (and attitude) will not accomplish what I want for them. My children do not need my disdain for who they are to motivate them to respect me and change their ways.

The Lord served in love and guided with His word. In love, He pointed out sin and invited them to change. Not a rigorous ruler, but a loving leader. We have the potential to be a loving leader just like our Lord.

Face to Face With Your Lord

Have a Conversation with Your Lord Jesus

🕊 Lord, who have you placed under my authority?

_____
_____

🕊 Lord, in what ways do I rule with rigor?

_____
_____

🕊 Lord, in what ways do I act towards others that show you are my Lord?

_____
_____

🕊 Lord, I do not want to treat people or my family with rigor. Please help me to find your way of leading and guiding. Please help me to be a loving leader.

*Pray...*_____

_____
                                        ...listen

CONVERSATION 61

My Friend, My Reproach

Related Bible Passages			
Old Testament	Psalms	Proverbs	New Testament
Leviticus 26	55	2	Luke 23

There are people in our life that we expect to criticize us. They are not our close friends, and history has proven them to be the ones who will be critical of our choices. Everyone has these people in their life -- the overly critical "advisor" we keep at a distance for safety.

But it is a bitter pill when a trusted, close friend corrects or criticizes you. You did not expect it and the criticism feels like a knife to your heart.

Psalm 55:12-14 For *it was* not an enemy *that* reproached me; then I could have borne *it*: neither *was it* he that hated me *that* did magnify *himself* against me; then I would have hid myself from him: But *it was* thou, a man mine equal, my guide, and mine acquaintance. We took sweet counsel together, *and* walked unto the house of God in company.

Your equal, your guide, your friend, maybe a fellow church member corrected you! It hurt, and it hurt really bad. What are you going to do now?

At this point, you may want to retreat. You cannot look at your friend in the eye and you do not want to be near her. You may feel the desire to escape the situation because of the tension.

> **Psalm 55:6-8** And I said, Oh that I had wings like a dove! *for then* would I fly away, and be at rest. Lo, *then* would I wander far off, *and* remain in the wilderness. Selah. I would hasten my escape from the windy storm *and* tempest.

The Lord put these passages into my life at just the right time. I was having difficulty processing some criticism that I had received. It had hurt and I was not sure why I was injured so deeply. The Lord helped me to see that it was because the criticism had come from my friend; someone that I deeply respected.

Many women who have been in this situation decide to retreat. They flee to the wilderness to protect themselves from further correction and criticism. If this situation happens within the church, then the criticized one might not enter the church doors again. Sadly, I know a handful of women that were hurt within the church walls and they fled into the "wilderness," never to return to the scene of the crime. Sad.

In my prayer over these passages, the Lord presented these questions. What if the correction was needed? Can't a friend tell you what you need to hear? What should you do with the pain that you feel?

First of all, correction is not always from a good source. We have those critical people in our life that will correct us every chance they get. In contrast, we have friends; friends that care and want to redirect us when they see us heading in the wrong direction. We must pray for wisdom to know the difference between the two.

> **Proverbs 2:12** To deliver thee from the way of the evil *man*, from the man that speaketh froward things;

No matter the source, we need to test the criticism to know if it is valid or not. We need to ask ourselves, "Does this correction seek to benefit me, or does the correction benefit the one offering the criticism?" If someone wants you to change to make things better for her, then she is speaking "forward things" and her words come from a selfish motivation.

A prime example of this is when the Lord Jesus was accused. His accusers wanted Him dead because He was getting in their way. The accusations they posed were to benefit them.

> **Luke 23:2** And they began to accuse him, saying, We found this *fellow* perverting the nation, and forbidding to give tribute to Caesar, saying that he himself is Christ a King.

> **Luke 23:10** And the chief priests and scribes stood and vehemently accused him.

The Lord showed me that I need correction in my life to grow closer to Christ. I will have things in my life that need fixing and redirection. Who better to deliver it than one who loves me -- a friend. Through my conversation with the Lord,

He revealed to me that this is why the pain was so intense. It hurt when my friend corrected me, but it was needful. Her criticism sought to make me better. My friend saw things that my eyes did not see. The friend that corrected me is the friend that can heal me if I will let her.

We need to walk together with our friends; pulling and correcting each other back to the path that leads to a closer relationship with the Lord; helping each other walk in God's statutes.

> **Leviticus 26:3-4** If ye walk in my statutes, and keep my commandments, and do them; Then I will give you rain in due season, and the land shall yield her increase, and the trees of the field shall yield their fruit.

> **Leviticus 26:6** And I will give peace in the land, and ye shall lie down, and none shall make *you* afraid: and I will rid evil beasts out of the land, neither shall the sword go through your land.

When we allow a friend to correct us then we can both enjoy "peace in the land." We can help each other to identify the "beasts" in each other's lives and help run them out. We need to take the correction and not fly away into the "wilderness." *We need to* rejoin hands with our friends. We need to take sweet counsel together and walk into the house of God in harmony.

Conversations

Have a Conversation with Your Lord Jesus

☙ Lord, do I prayerfully offer suggestions and correction to my friends? Am I willing to do this?

_____
_____
_____

☙ Lord, how did I react when a friend corrected me?

_____
_____
_____

☙ Lord, is there a friend that I pushed away because she corrected me?

_____
_____
_____

☙ Lord, I want you to use me to help my friends. Help me be kind as I offer guidance. Lord, I want to be better than I am and I want help from my friends. Help me to receive their correction and not push them away.

*Pray...*_____
_____
_____*...listen*

Face to Face With Your Lord

CONVERSATION 62

I Promise

Related Bible Passages			
Old Testament	Psalms	Proverbs	New Testament
Leviticus 27	56	3	Luke 24

You have heard it said that a promise is a promise. You also know how important it is that you keep your promises. The way you fulfill your promises not only affects your family, but it also will have an effect on your relationship with your Lord.

Psalm 56:12 Thy vows *are* upon me, O God: I will render praises unto thee.

Consider two different ways people offer promises. Some people are very cautious about making promises. They do not promise something unless they know they can deliver. Others carelessly make promises to pacify a family member with no plan or intention of seeing it through.

In my conversation with the Lord about promises that I have made to Him and others, He helped me understand that the way I care for the promises I make will relate to how seriously I consider God's promises. If I operate in the realm that "a promise is a promise" then it will be easy for me to believe and hope in God's promises. If I use my promises to pacify a needy family member with no plan to carry it through, then I might inadvertently assume that God does the same thing for me when it comes to His promises. I had not previously thought of the relationship between these two elements. It made me consider how careful am I with the promises I make.

Do you have a hard time believing in God's promises? Do you tend to forget what He has promised you? You can have a total abiding confidence in your Lord. He will attend to every promise fully and will not let you fall into a trap. You can know without a doubt. Your Lord is with you!

> **Proverbs 3:26** For the LORD shall be thy confidence, and shall keep thy foot from being taken.

In Leviticus, we learn more about the laws governing offerings. When a man is bringing the offering to the Lord, he cannot change it to suit himself or his situation; it cannot be changed to suit his circumstances. Relating this to our promises, we should not change our vow to suit our current situation. If we promised to do something, we must give the effort to do it exactly as we said to the extent that we are able.

> **Leviticus 27:9-10** And if *it be* a beast, whereof men bring an offering unto the LORD, all that *any man* giveth of such unto the LORD shall be holy. He shall not alter it, nor change it, a good for a bad, or a bad for a good: and if he shall at all change beast for beast, then it and the exchange thereof shall be holy.

Don't we depend on this pattern from the Lord? Don't we want His promises to be exactly as He promised with no changes based on the situation? Don't we want to believe and KNOW that He will do what He has promised?

There is great peace in knowing that God's promises are sure. If you don't have that peace, could it be because of how you follow through on the promises you make?

Even Christ's disciples needed to be reminded of what the Lord had promised. After His death, His disciples encountered two angels.

> **Luke 24:5-6** And as they were afraid, and bowed down *their* faces to the earth, they said unto them, Why seek ye the living among the dead? He is not here, but is risen: <u>remember how he spake unto you</u> when he was yet in Galilee,

The angles had to jog their memory. He had promised many wonderful things to them, but they had forgotten. Through this conversation, I learned that if my promises are released carelessly and can be changed based on how I am feeling, then I might have a hard time believing that God's promises are sure and unconditional. If I don't take my promises seriously, it will be hard for me to take God's promises seriously.

I can't imagine living a life where I can't count on God's promises toward me. They are a key to my security in God and a cornerstone to my faith. We need to keep our promises dear, precious, and certain, so we can easily relate to how God considers His promises toward us.

Face to Face With Your Lord

Have a Conversation with Your Lord Jesus

☙ Lord, what are some promises you have made me?

_____

_____

☙ Lord, what are some promises I have made to others but have not honored?

_____

_____

☙ Lord, do I doubt your promises? Do I believe that you will not honor your word?

_____

_____

☙ Lord, show me where I doubt you. Help me to know your promises and then believe what you have said. Lord help me to honor my promises the way you honor your promises.

*Pray...*_____

_____

...listen

CONVERSATION 63

Safe in the Camp of the Lord

Related Bible Passages			
Old Testament	**Psalms**	**Proverbs**	**New Testament**
Numbers 1	57	4	John 1

Imagine the camp of the early Israelites. In their great multitude, there was order. In the center of the camp was the tabernacle and in every direction from the tabernacle were the tribes of Israel organized into family groups. The camp provided the families with physical safety as well as spiritual safety.

As the saying goes, "there is safety in numbers," and this was true for the Israelites. They were a formidable force against any attack. But the camp also provided spiritual safety. Being part of a group all serving the same God helped to keep each individual spiritually accountable and focused on keeping the right spirit.

If an Israelite decided to leave the camp and go out on his own, he would suddenly find himself vulnerable to physical and spiritual attack. This wanderer would still be an Israelite - a child of God - but living without the physical and spiritual protection that the camp provided.

As I was having this conversation with the Lord, I asked Him about the people I have known that had wandered. I could remember one particular person that had walked away from the church community and from a desire to serve the Lord. I had to wonder why she would leave. Why did she suddenly see the "camp" as a threat? It seemed that the smallest offense had caused her to run. As I continued to read and talk with the Lord, a possible progression of events emerged.

The Lord showed me that this individual might have forgotten what brought her into the camp in the first place. She was brought into the "camp" the day she received God's forgiveness for her sins. She followed the invitation from the Lord Jesus to come "follow me."

> **John 1:43** The day following Jesus would go forth into Galilee, and findeth Philip, and saith unto him, Follow me.

After receiving the Lord's forgiveness, she found herself amongst others within this camp of believers and she felt and knew the nearness of the Lord. She reaped the benefit of being in fellowship with other Christians. They helped her, guided her, and supported her. She felt protected and safe. She could not imagine ever leaving the camp and leaving the fellowship of the Lord and His people.

Psalm 57:7 My heart is fixed, O God, my heart is fixed: I will sing and give praise.

But then something happened. Maybe God's word or God's people reproved and corrected her. She felt hurt and wounded. In order to protect herself from further injury, she concluded that she should leave the camp. The problem was that she was focused on self-preservation instead of growth. She did not recognize that sometimes pain is involved in growth and keeping her spiritually and emotionally healthy. Instead of seeking healing and support from within the camp, she believed that the only place she could heal was outside of the camp; away from those that caused her injury, and pain.

In the fog of self-preservation, she was failing to see that by leaving the camp she was walking into danger. Outside the camp, there was no one to help her spiritually, no one to help guide her spirit, no Word to light her path. She found herself alone and surrounded by darkness.

Proverbs 4:14-15 Enter not into the path of the wicked, and go not in the way of evil *men*. Avoid it, pass not by it, turn from it, and pass away.

Contrary to what she might believe, there was no healing outside of the camp. Her wounds would not heal when she was walking without the Word. She might have come to the conclusion that separation was best, but she was creating more spiritual harm. The only way for her to heal was to go back to the camp. Let reproof and correction fall upon her like a healing salve. She needed to let God's people and the Lord's presence heal and guide her in the right way.

The Lord helped me to see that the pain of reproof is what caused her to flee. This conversation convinced me that when I feel the pain of reproof, I shouldn't run to the outskirts of the camp. I should run to the center of the camp, and closer to people that love and serve Him.

So, where are you in the camp? Have you thought about leaving the camp of the Lord? In other words, separating yourself from other Christians because you have been offended, or someone failed to meet your expectations?

> **Numbers 1:18** And they assembled all the congregation together on the first *day* of the second month, and they declared their pedigrees after their families, by the house of their fathers, according to the number of the names, from twenty years old and upward, by their polls.

If you were to stand up and declare your association or your current position in the "camp", what would you say? "I belong to the camp of Self-Fulfillment!", "I belong to the camp of Bitterness!" Or, "I belong to the camp of the Lord, and safely will I reside!"

Conversations

Have a Conversation with Your Lord Jesus

🕮 Lord, am I seeking to escape from your camp and from your people?

_____
_____

🕮 Lord, if I am seeking to wander from the camp, what am I hoping to find?

_____
_____

🕮 Lord, when I am content to reside in the camp, what benefits do I experience from your people and from your word?

_____
_____

🕮 Lord, I need to reside in your camp. I know I need your people. Please help me to get rid of thoughts that convince me that I don't need you, your word, or your people.

Pray... _____

_____ *...listen*

Face to Face With Your Lord

CONVERSATION 64

I Got to See it Happen

Related Bible Passages			
Old Testament	Psalms	Proverbs	New Testament
Numbers 3	58	5	John 2

You win trophies for being first in a race. You win prizes to recognize your performance in an event. You gain recognition for performing well on the job. While these awards are a great symbol of your effort, there is a reward that I want most. It is the one that comes from dedicated service to the Lord, and the reward for serving Him is getting to see Him work in amazing ways.

In my Bible reading, I saw that the Levites were set aside for service to the Lord.

Numbers 3:6-7 Bring the tribe of Levi near, and present them before Aaron the priest, that they may minister unto him. And they shall keep his charge, and the charge of the whole congregation before the tabernacle of the congregation, to do the service of the tabernacle.

Their service was not glamorous or easy, but it was specifically for the Lord. They received a specific direction from the Lord and He picked them to do the job. What an honor! I am certain that being in that position, so close to the tabernacle and the priest, they had the privilege to witness the wonderful workings of the Lord. Being this close to the action they got to see things others missed.

As I thought about this passage, I started talking to the Lord about the many wonderful things that I been able to see Him do. Being a pastor's wife, I get to be close to the action and have seen God's hand work in our lives and in the lives of others. The same is true for you. When you are serving close to the Lord, you get to witness amazing things. Consider the servants at the wedding in Cana.

> **John 2:9** When the ruler of the feast had tasted the water that was made wine, and knew not whence it was: (but the servants which drew the water knew;) the governor of the feast called the bridegroom,

Serving close to Jesus, the servants got to witness a miracle. I can hear them now. "Did you see that? Did you see what He just did! That was amazing! I can't believe that I got to see that!" Those few servants got to see the Lord do something amazing that was lost to the rest of the party.

Have you been close to someone serving in the ministry? Listen to a missionary talk about his experiences while on the field or listen to a pastor talk about how the Lord led and directed him. You will see that there is a great reward for those that are close to the Lord and serving Him. When you are serving close to the Lord, you will get see Him work in someone's life and intervene in a miraculous way. You will get to say, "Wow, I can't believe I got to see that happen. God is amazing!"

Psalm 58:11 So that a man shall say, Verily *there is* a reward for the righteous: verily he is a God that judgeth in the earth.

So where are you serving? Are you serving close to the Lord? When we decide to serve with the Lord, we will see great rewards because we will witness the great things that the Lord does. We will know the truth about many things that will be missed by the rest of the world. We have many "good" things to do associated with being a wife, mother, caretaker, and homemaker, but don't neglect service with the Lord.

Proverbs 5:10 Lest strangers be filled with thy wealth; and thy labours *be* in the house of a stranger;

We need to get close to the Lord and work alongside Him to accomplish something amazing; hand out tracts, lead a Bible study, clean the church, visit the homebound. Serving in any capacity will bring great reward because we will have the opportunity to see the work of our amazing Lord.

There is a great reward for the righteous. There is a great reward for the servant of the Lord. Servants get to see some amazing things.

Face to Face With Your Lord

Have a Conversation with Your Lord

🔖 Lord, how am I serving close to you?

_____
_____

🔖 Lord, what are some amazing things I have seen you do?

_____
_____

🔖 Lord, what are some other ways I can serve you and get closer?

_____
_____

🔖 Lord, I want to see amazing things. I want to see evidence of your hand in my life and in the lives of others. Help me to stay close to you and serve close to you.

*Pray...*_____

_____
_____*...listen*

Face to Face with Your Lord

CONVERSATION 65

Boundaries and Walls

	Related Bible Passages		
Old Testament	Psalms	Proverbs	New Testament
Numbers 4	59	6	John 3

Boundaries, borders, rules, snares, walls: these are words that we use to describe how our lives can be limited or hindered. Sometimes they are good and meant for our protection. Other times they are self-imposed by the decisions we make.

The book of Numbers is filled with rules and laws. The people were guided by these rules. The rules gave their community order and also helped the people to understand their God. While these rules and laws were numerous, they served a purpose in teaching and instructing the people. In fact, today you can look at some of those rules and appreciate the wisdom the Lord had in setting those limits.

> **Numbers 4:15** And when Aaron and his sons have made an end of covering the sanctuary, and all the vessels of the sanctuary, as the camp is to set forward; after that, the sons of Kohath shall come to bear *it*: but they shall not touch *any* holy thing, lest they die. These *things are* the burden of the sons of Kohath in the tabernacle of the congregation.

The Lord also uses boundaries to protect us from getting hurt, but only if we willingly live within those boundaries.

> **Psalm 59:1** Deliver me from mine enemies, O my God: defend me from them that rise up against me.

> **Psalm 59:9** *Because of* his strength will I wait upon thee: for God *is* my defence.

As I had this conversation with the Lord about boundaries He has placed in my life, He reminded me that as a parent I wanted a fence around the yard to prevent my children from going too far from home. I wanted the fence to protect them from harm. The Lord will put forth boundaries that will protect me from danger. However, the Lord also showed me that there are some boundaries or snares that are self-imposed and not a part of His plan.

> **Proverbs 6:1-2** My son, if thou be surety for thy friend, *if* thou hast stricken thy hand with a stranger, Thou art snared with the words of thy mouth, thou art taken with the words of thy mouth.

> **Proverbs 6:5** Deliver thyself as a roe from the hand *of the hunter*, and as a bird from the hand of the fowler.

The Lord reminded me that I need to be careful about what promises or agreements I make with others. I am snared by my own words. My words have the potential to create a self-imposed wall (or obligation) in my life. The only way around this wall is through the door of fulfilling the promise I made.

People will hold us to what we say! It is not bad to make promises, but we need to always remember that it is a snare in which we willingly insert ourselves. It is something from which we have to deliver ourselves.

One of the most formidable walls is found in the book of John where Jesus is talking about how a man can get to see Heaven. This wall cannot be penetrated by your power; you cannot go around this wall. This wall will prevent your eternal home in heaven if you do not follow God's way of getting past this barrier.

John 3:3 Jesus answered and said unto him, Verily, verily, I say unto thee, Except a man be born again, he cannot see the kingdom of God.

This is a boundary with NO exceptions! The only way to have a home in heaven is to be born again; receiving Jesus Christ's gift of salvation from the penalty of your sins. There is no other way! God will not remove this boundary for you or let you go around it in another way. How do you experience a new birth? You become born again by asking Jesus to forgive you for your sins and by faith ask Him to give you His righteousness. Being a good person is not how you get "born again" and doing good things will not get you past this wall. If you do not get past this wall you "cannot see the kingdom of God!"

Freedom, choices, unhindered ambition: you hear that this is what makes a great life. You might believe that there is nothing to get in your way of pursuing your happiness. But as I get to know my Lord, I want His boundaries. I want His laws. I want Him to prevent me from doing something harmful. God's boundaries and laws do not stand in the way of our happiness. His boundaries and laws are a joy to heed. His boundaries and laws actually bring great happiness and security.

Conversations

Have a Conversation with Your Lord Jesus

☙ Lord, what boundaries have you placed in my life?

_____
_____

☙ Lord, how have I stepped beyond those boundaries and what were the consequences?

_____
_____

☙ Lord, how have I despised your boundaries? Why have you placed them in my life?

_____
_____

☙ Lord, I place myself within your boundaries willingly. I know they give me safety, protection, and understanding. Thank you for loving me enough to put boundaries in my life.

*Pray...*_____

_____
...listen

Face to Face With Your Lord

CONVERSATION 66

Rise and Shine

Related Bible Reading			
Old Testament	Psalms	Proverbs	New Testament
Numbers 6	60	7	John 4

As she lays in bed contemplating her day ahead, she feels exhausted before her feet ever hit the floor. It all seems overwhelming; so much to do and no opportunity to get it done. The demands on her were coming from all directions. As she takes a deep breath of defeat, she feels a twinge of bitterness as she reaches for her Bible. It feels as if it is a burden to spend some of her precious time on this required task. The thought, "This does no good; I am wasting my time," begins to form in the back of her mind.

As she opens her Bible and starts to read, a passage she skims across grabs her attention:

> Proverbs 7:24 Hearken unto me now therefore, O ye children, and attend to the words of my mouth.

Her interest is slightly awakened. She wonders if God could possibly have something for her today. She knows she is needing something to make it through another day, but can help really come from the book she is holding in her lap? She can feel the dryness of her spirit and giving up is just a step away. She suppresses those feelings and decides to keep reading and watching the words on the page for encouragement or a message from the Lord. She fumbles through the pages looking for another passage, and she pauses to read:

> **John 4:14** But whosoever drinketh of the water that I shall give him shall never thirst; but the water that I shall give him shall be in him a well of water springing up into everlasting life.

The passage instantly resonates with her condition. "That is it. I think I am thirsty!" She knows that her spirit is dry, cracked, and barren. It has been a long time since she has reached for her Bible. It has been a while since she has had a meaningful conversation with God. As she holds her Bible, she thinks back to a time when she was excited to open her Bible and capture something new from the Lord. She remembers walking down the street talking to Him.

She pauses and meditates on this verse and how it relates to how she is feeling. She slowly realizes that refreshment does not come from accomplishment; refreshment comes from the Lord Jesus. It comes from pressing into Him and getting closer to Him.

But how can she get back to that point? How will she be able to rekindle that relationship? Errantly she believes that it would take an unimaginable effort to get back to the Lord when in reality a simple prayer of confession and forgiveness would bring the nearness back. By not acknowledging this fact, anxiety rushes over her as she falsely believes a great gulf exists between her and God. As she thinks about this, the feelings of defeat begin to well up again. Trying to hold onto the idea that the Lord will refresh, she flips to another passage and picks a few more verses to read.

> **Numbers 6:24-26** The LORD bless thee, and keep thee: The LORD make his face shine upon thee, and be gracious unto thee: The LORD lift up his countenance upon thee, and give thee peace.

The words within this verse shot off the page and she has to read them again. She knows the Lord is trying to get her attention. "The *Lord* keeps me! I was thinking that I had to try to get back to Him, but He is actually holding on to me. *He* keeps me!" She realizes that she has been trying to do God's job and it was exhausting. She has been trying to get close to Him through doing good, laboring and striving. She realizes that she had finally given up because God seemed unattainable.

She understands now that her motive is what is exhausting her. Laboring to attain God's favor leads to defeat. Laboring out of gratitude and love is refreshing! Trying to attain the unattainable will not last long. Serving out of gratitude will last forever.

She feels a rush of refreshment come over her as she realizes the Lord Jesus Christ is near and He is keeping her close to Him. All she has to do is just reach out. A sense of love and gratitude for her wonderful Lord rushes over her.

God keeps her and her expression of love and gratitude is all she needs to keep her heart near to Him. She takes a moment to close her eyes and relax into her Lord. She tells Him that she is glad He is near and that she is sorry for doubting

His presence. Now, with her relationship with the Lord reunited, she still feels the pressure from the day ahead. She can still feel the dread of life and knowing she has to face it alone makes it worse. Before she leaves her bed, she decides to flip to one last passage in her Bible.

> **Psalm 60:11-12** Give us help from trouble: for vain *is* the help of man. Through God we shall do valiantly: for he *it is that* shall tread down our enemies.

Tears start to well up in her eyes as she now sees that the Lord wants her to know that He is with her throughout her day. He is fighting for her. She is not alone. He gives her help. Not only is her Lord *keeping* her, but He is also *fighting* for her!

What an amazing morning she has had with the Lord. She opened her Bible with a sense of resentment, and she is now closing it with a sense of refreshment. She knows God is real and very near and is speaking directly to her this morning. As her feet hit the floor, she is still in awe of what she has just experienced. She heard God this morning!

Conversations

Have a Conversation with Your Lord Jesus

☙ Lord, when I open my Bible, is it out of duty or out of anticipation?

_____
_____
_____

☙ Lord, do I let myself be refreshed by your words?

_____
_____
_____

☙ Lord, what is my motive? Am I laboring to prove myself to you or am I focused on showing my gratitude?

_____
_____
_____

☙ Lord, I am looking forward to my time with you. I anticipate a message from you and I know you will speak to me. I know that you love me and keep me!

*Pray...*_____
_____
_____*...listen*

Face to Face With Your Lord

Face to Face with Your Lord

CONVERSATION 67

Bethesda

	Related Bible Reading		
Old Testament	Psalms	Proverbs	New Testament
Numbers 7	61	8	John 5

He lived beside Bethesda every day. He was always watching and waiting for the water to move.

John 5:4 For an angel went down at a certain season into the pool, and troubled the water: whosoever then first after the troubling of the water stepped in was made whole of whatsoever disease he had.

He had seen it happen, but while he was slowly making my way to the pool, someone would step down before him. He had been lame for 38 years. Oh, how he wanted to be healed!

Sitting at the pool he would cry out to God. His heart was overwhelmed. He begged God to trouble the water and to heal him. He would cry out with painful tears *"...lead me to the rock that is higher than I." (Psalm 61:2)*

While sitting there he would think back to Moses' time. The princes brought their offering before the Lord on their day. One spoon of gold full of incense; one young bullock, one ram, one lamb of the first year; for a burnt offering. One kid of the goats for a sin offering. Day after day the same thing. But when Moses went into the tabernacle, he heard the voice of God speaking to him from the ark.

He believed that in his mundane life, God could still appear and speak to him just as he had spoken to Moses. Day after day he sat, watching and anticipating that the Lord would help him. He knew that God would come for him; he had faith that the Lord would not leave him. He couldn't let something distract him. He didn't want to miss seeing that water move. He didn't want to miss his opportunity. He didn't want to miss his God.

Then one day, He came. Jesus. The man heard His voice just like Moses did in the tabernacle. Jesus saw him by the pool and said, "Rise, take up thy bed, and walk." (John 5:8)

Glory! Immediately he knew he was healed. It was just like he had imagined. Instantly he had strength, and energy and a compulsion to leap! He was healed! Jesus healed him!

He often thinks what might have become of him if he had not been faithfully watching. He was in the right place at the right time watching for the water to move and he got to see Jesus Christ. He got to feel the hand of God.

He doesn't go to the pool of Bethesda anymore. He has no need. But he has not ceased to watch and wait; anticipating for the Lord to move again. Just because he has been healed, doesn't mean that he should stop watching, waiting, and anticipating the Lord to "trouble the water." He still watches for the Lord and looks forward to hearing His voice and direction. You see, Jesus told him, "Behold, thou art made whole: sin no more, lest a worse thing come unto thee." (John 5:14)

Jesus healed him, but he understands that it is his job to keep himself from becoming "lame" again. Sin will make him spiritually lame. If he gets distracted and loses his attention, then he could inadvertently allow sin into his life and become spiritually lame. He had been physically lame, and he knew that pain all too well. Being spiritually lame and sick would be a worse thing. He must never let this happen.

"Oh Lord, I have my eyes on you! Lord, you have my focus and attention. I am watching you like I was watching the water," he declares to the Lord.

> **Proverbs 8:34-35** Blessed *is* the man that heareth me, watching daily at my gates, waiting at the posts of my doors. For whoso findeth me findeth life, and shall obtain favour of the LORD.

"When I read your word, I am watching, waiting, and anticipating you to move. When I hear your word preached, I am watching, waiting, and anticipating you to move. When I am simply going through my day, I am watching, waiting, and anticipating you to move. I don't want to miss you, Lord. I don't want to miss you when you trouble the water again."

Bethesda is always with him. In his heart, he still lives beside Bethesda in the way that he approaches his life. Over and over he now sees how the Lord moves and performs amazing things.

Do you live beside Bethesda? Are you watching for the Lord to move? Has the Lord troubled the water and you missed it because you were not paying attention? When the Lord moves, it is miraculous, and you don't want to miss it!

Live life like you are living beside Bethesda.

Face to Face With Your Lord

Have a Conversation with Your Lord Jesus

🕊 Lord, is my attention on you?

_____
_____

🕊 Lord, what is my distraction? What takes my eyes off of you?

_____
_____

🕊 Lord, have I become spiritually lame?

_____
_____

🕊 Lord, I want to live beside Bethesda. I want to have my attention on you throughout the day waiting for you to "trouble the waters."

*Pray...*_____
_____
                                                    ...listen

CONVERSATION 68

Wait

Related Bible Reading			
Old Testament	Psalms	Proverbs	New Testament
Numbers 9	62	9	John 6

Doctrinally, we know that the Lord is with us and will never forsake us. We know that He wants the best for us and will lead us in the right direction if we are yielded. But the hard part is to wait; to wait on the Lord to give us direction.

By definition, "wait" means to stay where one is or delay action until a particular time or until something else happens. This has to be one of the hardest things to learn as a Christian – to wait for the Lord.

The Israelites had to wait. Traveling through the wilderness, they had to keep their eye on the cloud that abode upon the tabernacle. When it moved, they moved. If it didn't move, they didn't move.

Numbers 9:18-19 At the commandment of the LORD the children of Israel journeyed, and at the commandment of the LORD they pitched: as long as the cloud abode upon the tabernacle they rested in their tents. And when the cloud tarried long upon the tabernacle many days, then the children of Israel kept the charge of the LORD, and journeyed not.

I can imagine that it must have been difficult when the cloud "tarried long upon the tabernacle." Each day they would wake up and look at the cloud. "Nope, no movement. I guess we just wait." Day after day of waiting one might start to wonder if the "cloud" was just a cloud. When the cloud tarried long upon the tabernacle many days, it might have been easy to assume that the Lord was no longer present because of the absence of movement.

As I am writing this conversation, the Lord is having me to wait. This conversation came at the perfect time in my life. We are having to make a major decision for our family and are needing some specific direction from the Lord. In light of no instant answer from the Lord, we have to wait. It is hard. I want to start planning but with no movement from the Lord, I have to wait.

There are times in our life where the Lord needs us to wait -- *wait until a particular time or until something else happens.* Each day we wake up and nothing new from the Lord happens. We should not let this make us think the Lord has "left the cloud." If you are in a time of your life where the Lord is having you wait, then wait. Watch and wait for Him to move. Know that He is still there when "nothing" is happening.

In Proverbs 9, Solomon shows that a process is necessary for accomplishing a task.

> **Proverbs 9:1-2** Wisdom hath builded her house, she hath hewn out her seven pillars: She hath killed her beasts; she hath mingled her wine; she hath also furnished her table.

First things first. Through this conversation, the Lord has shown me that I can't rush the process or the Lord's hand. He will move when He is ready. I should not be fooled into believing that He is no longer there just because I have not seen Him move. The devil would love to get me to believe that my God has left me and caused me to take matters into my own hands.

> **Psalm 62:1** Truly my soul waiteth upon God: from him *cometh* my salvation.

Have you gotten tired of waiting for the Lord to move? Have you started to believe that He has left you? Are you faced with an impossible situation and you need to see the Lord, NOW!!?

In my conversation with the Lord, He had me consider the situation that Philip was placed in by the Lord Jesus. The Lord was surrounded by 5,000 hungry people.

> **John 6:5-7** When Jesus then lifted up *his* eyes, and saw a great company come unto him, he saith unto Philip, Whence shall we buy bread, that these may eat? And this he said to prove him: for he himself knew what he would do. Philip answered him, Two hundred pennyworth of bread is not sufficient for them, that every one of them may take a little.

I can imagine the feeling of sheer panic that Philip felt as he considered the task asked of him. The part of this passage that stood out to me was "...for he himself knew what he would do." Jesus was in control. He knew exactly what He was going to do. Philip needed to be obedient.

This conversation could not have happened at a better time. It was exactly what I needed. I need to wait for the Lord. He knows what He is going to do in my situation.

Do you believe that this is true in your life? Do you believe that the Lord knows what He is going to do? If the Lord knows what He is going to do, then your job is to wait. Wait for the Lord to move and enjoy watching the miracle.

Have a Conversation with Your Lord Jesus

☙ Lord, is there something for which you are having me to wait?

_____
_____

☙ Lord, in what ways have I stepped ahead of you to create the solution rather than waiting for the miracle?

_____
_____

☙ Lord, have I started to believe that you have forgotten about intervening in my situation?

_____
_____

☙ Lord, I want to wait for you to move in my life. May I not step ahead of you in this situation, but truly wait for an answer from you.

*Pray...*_____

_____
_____*...listen*

Face to Face With Your Lord

CONVERSATION 69

You Can be a Prophet

Related Bible Passages			
Old Testament	Psalms	Proverbs	New Testament
Numbers 11	63	10	John 7

This world needs more prophets. Not prophets in the sense of foretelling of things to come, but prophets that will "tell-forth" the word of God. Moses saw the need for more prophets.

> **Numbers 11:27-29** And there ran a young man, and told Moses, and said, Eldad and Medad do prophesy in the camp. And Joshua the son of Nun, the servant of Moses, *one* of his young men, answered and said, My lord Moses, forbid them. And Moses said unto him, Enviest thou for my sake? would God that all the LORD'S people were prophets, *and* that the LORD would put his spirit upon them!

This was Moses' desire. He was not threatened by others being led by God and speaking on God's behalf. He saw great value in others speaking for the Lord. Every Christian has the potential to speak for the Lord and pass His message on. As I started reading the passages above, I had to wonder if I diligently pray and seek opportunities to speak for the Lord? Do I act as a prophet?

I believe this world needs women that will speak of God and tell other thirsty souls of His love. Am I willing to be one of those prophets? Will I pray for the Lord's spirit to be upon me, so I can tell others? I realized this was grossly missing in my life!

> **Psalm 63:1** O God, thou *art* my God; early will I seek thee: my soul thirsteth for thee, my flesh longeth for thee in a dry and thirsty land, where no water is;

In order to be a prophet, we must have something to tell. In order to have something to tell, we have to receive the message from the Lord. In order to receive this message, our soul must thirst for God's touch and then be ready to receive His word. Nothing is more meaningful or powerful. Having the Lord touch and direct our life is a wonderful thing. If we are willing to be a prophet, we will eagerly seek the Lord early and thirst after His direction. When this happens, we will have something to tell others.

As I was having this conversation with the Lord, I had to pause and wonder, when I speak, what do others hear me talking about? People listen to my words and come to understand what is important to me. They listen to in hopes of capturing something that they can use. What about you? When you speak, what do others hear you talking about?

John 7:18 He that speaketh of himself seeketh his own glory: but he that seeketh his glory that sent him, the same is true, and no unrighteousness is in him.

Are you talking about what you have accomplished for the day (glory to you), or are you talking about what the Lord has accomplished IN YOU (glory to God)?

We need to develop a desire to be a prophet and tell others of God's amazing works and of His amazing works in us. We need to seek God's direction and let Him lead us to speak for Him. May we have the privilege to feed many with His message and with our experiences with our Lord. May we be sensitive to His words, so we have something to say and feed those starving for His love.

Proverbs 10:21 The lips of the righteous feed many: but fools die for want of wisdom.

Face to Face With Your Lord

Have a Conversation with Your Lord Jesus

🕊 Lord, am I a prophet for you?

_____
_____

🕊 Lord, how often do I speak of you?

_____
_____

🕊 Lord, do I seek you early to gain inspiration and words to pass on to others?

_____
_____

🕊 Lord, I want to be a prophet and have a desire to tell others of your amazing works. I want to have the privilege to feed many with your message.

*Pray...*_____
_____
_____*...listen*

Face to Face with Your Lord

CONVERSATION 70

Help Me

	Related Bible Passages		
Old Testament	**Psalms**	**Proverbs**	**New Testament**
Numbers 13	64	11	John 8

In order to survive this life, we must have help, advice, and direction from others. However, sometimes we wait too long to seek it. If you are like other women, you might convince yourself that you can survive on your own or maybe you are too embarrassed to ask for help believing that you might be shamed for asking. For many reasons and excuses, sometimes it is so hard to ask for advice. We have to swallow our pride, we have to know who to turn to, and we have to be ready to hear the direction.

As I started my conversation with the Lord, He pointed out to me how I resist asking for help. In my conversation, I threw out the excuses that I want to be self-sufficient and capable, I don't want to be a burden, and I don't want to seem needy. The Lord quickly showed me how those excuses were self-serving and insulting to those that do right and ask for help. Through the verses above He showed me how I really do need the hand of others in my life.

The Lord never intended for me to walk through this life alone. I am to reach out to others to help them along; I am to be ready with an answer when someone comes to me for help. However, it is also true that I am to seek help and receive advice from others. This is God's plan. Sometimes God needs an audible voice and He needs physical, loving hands. He will use someone in my life to be that voice and be those hands when I am ready.

Are you willing to seek counsel; are you willing to cry out for help?

Proverbs 11:14 Where no counsel *is,* the people fall: but in the multitude of counsellers *there is* safety.

Are you facing a major decision? Seek counsel. Are you struggling with something that seems so small? Seek counsel. Talk with a trust-worthy Christian lady and let her be a voice of wisdom in your life. God may need her to communicate something special to you or use her to give you a comforting hug. Seek counsel.

Walking through this life can be very confusing. We have no ability to see into the future, but through the guidance of an older, wiser, woman we might just get a glimpse of the future through her eyes. She has lived beyond our years and she can help us avoid things that we will not know to avoid. God can use other people to give us direction, but we have to seek counsel to hear it.

The Lord Jesus was teaching the Jews and helping them to understand that if they would follow His teachings, then they will grow, know the truth and find fulfillment.

John 8:31-32 Then said Jesus to those Jews which believed on him, If ye continue in my word, *then* are ye my disciples indeed; And ye shall know the truth, and the truth shall make you free.

However, this truth does not fully exist in its entirety within us. We have to seek what we don't know from an outside source. We need others to enhance our understanding of God's truth. Wise counsel can reveal secrets and make many things known to us. We should not be afraid to turn to a wise Christian and seek advice and direction.

As you seek counsel, you should be careful. Not every woman will give you good direction. A woman that is not prayerfully following the Lord will not have the wherewithal to give you Godly direction. When you seek counsel, you are looking for a direction that comes from the heart of God. After you seek direction, seek confirmation from your Bible. God's direction will never contradict His word.

Psalm 64:2-3 Hide me from the secret counsel of the wicked; from the insurrection of the workers of iniquity: Who whet their tongue like a sword, *and* bend *their bows to shoot* their arrows, *even* bitter words:

Be careful from whom you seek counsel. Bad advice can turn you in the wrong direction and could lead you to turn your back on God. It matters who you listen to! Consider the men that went to spy out the promised land for Moses.

Numbers 13:32 And they brought up an evil report of the land which they had searched unto the children of Israel, saying, The land, through which we have gone to search it, *is* a land that eateth up the inhabitants thereof; and all the people that we saw in it *are* men of a great stature.

Caleb brought a different report and "... stilled the people before Moses, and said, Let us go up at once, and possess it; for we are well able to overcome it." (Numbers 13:30)

One man brought the heart of God and counseled the people to follow God. Ten other men, motivated by fear, counseled the people to turn from God and His promises. We must be willing to seek advice and direction. We must be careful to whom we listen. A good counselor will point us toward God and His ways; she will be in tune with God and encourage our relationship with Him.

Conversations

Have a Conversation with Your Lord Jesus

✤ Lord, am I willing to ask for help and seek counsel?

_____
_____

✤ Lord, who are the people that I go to for advice?

_____
_____

✤ Lord, when have I listened to the wrong person and was led away from you?

_____
_____

✤ Lord, help me to swallow my pride and seek help. I know I don't have all the answers and need to hear your voice through others. Help me to have the wisdom to identify those from whom I should seek direction.

*Pray...*_____
_____
                                            ...listen

CONVERSATION 71

Glory to God

Related Bible Passages			
Old Testament	Psalms	Proverbs	New Testament
Numbers 14	65	12	John 9

When people rise up against you, your first reaction probably is to defend your honor and your intentions. But that very action, while very natural, is an effort to bring glory to you. Isn't your life supposed to be about bringing glory to God? In a situation where you are being challenged, this is a very difficult position to take. When you consider the sacrifice Jesus Christ made on the cross for you, bringing glory to Him out of pure gratitude is easy. But when your actions and integrity are challenged, will your motivation will be self-preservation, or finding a way to glorify God in the situation?

As I was reading the passages, I had to wonder what my response would be if people were talking against me. What would I do if others were wrongfully complaining about what

I am doing? Would I come out in self-defense and blame others for how I am being accused, or would I try to use the situation to bring God glory? I could sense the Lord asking me, "Are you willing to set your self-preservation aside you so that I can get the glory? Are you willing to let people verbally wound you and accuse you? Would you come to their defense before me or would you focus on defending yourself?"

> **Numbers 14:2** And all the children of Israel murmured against Moses and against Aaron: and the whole congregation said unto them, Would God that we had died in the land of Egypt! or would God we had died in this wilderness!

The Israelites despised Moses for leading them into this wilderness. However, they failed to recognize that it was their sin and their decision to not cross over into the promised land and that has placed them in the wilderness. They were filled with anger, dissatisfaction, and rebellion.

> **Numbers 14:11-12** And the LORD said unto Moses, How long will this people provoke me? and how long will it be ere they believe me, for all the signs which I have shewed among them? I will smite them with the pestilence, and disinherit them, and will make of thee a greater nation and mightier than they.

At this point, facing an angry mob of rebellious and angry Israelites, what would you have said to the Lord? If I was Moses, I think would have come to my defense and said, "Do what you must, Lord. Pestilence or boils would be good. Thank you, Lord, for coming to my defense. Thank you for delivering me!" But not Moses. He did not come to his own defense, he came to THEIR defense. He recognized that if the Israelites were destroyed it would not bring glory to God. His reputation as a great a powerful God would be tarnished. Moses was more concerned about God's reputation (God getting the glory) than his own self-preservation. Moses pleaded with God.

> **Numbers 14:15-16** Now *if* thou shalt kill *all* this people as one man, then the nations which have heard the fame of thee will speak, saying, Because the LORD was not able to bring this people into the land which he sware unto them, therefore he hath slain them in the wilderness.

> **Numbers 14:19-20** Pardon, I beseech thee, the iniquity of this people according unto the greatness of thy mercy, and as thou hast forgiven this people, from Egypt even until now. And the LORD said, I have pardoned according to thy word:

Through this situation, God was trying to reveal the essence of Moses' heart to Moses. In order to keep going in this position of leadership, Moses needed to have the heart-desire to preserve God's people over preserving himself, and Moses needed to acknowledge how he really felt about the Israelites. His reaction to God's threat proved to himself that he truly wanted God's glory to be seen and his self-preservation denied.

Through these verses, the Lord helped me to see that I need to have an increased heart-desire to preserve God's people rather than an inflated concern over my own self-preservation. I can put aside my desire to prove my own "righteousness" in order to preserve God's people and His work in their lives.

The fate of the Israelites might have rested in Moses' hands. Moses made a conscious decision to put God's heart before his own vindication and in doing so he preserved the lives of the Israelites. But what would have happened if Moses had not dug deep into his heart to squash self-preservation? What would have happened if Moses had said, "Yes, Lord destroy them all. I am sick of all this?" We will never know, but I am thankful that Moses was willing to seek the heart of God, bring Him glory and deny himself the gratification of vindication.

> **Psalm 65:2-3** O thou that hearest prayer, unto thee shall all flesh come. Iniquities prevail against me: *as for* our transgressions, thou shalt purge them away.

The Lord showed me that this is the most important thing -- that all flesh would come to the Lord. In order for this to happen, God must be glorified. Moses had been personally hurt and the people had spoken out against him, but he was not concerned about preserving his reputation. He was concerned about God getting and keeping the glory, and God having a good name among the nations so that all flesh would turn to Him. Moses received personal satisfaction from serving his Lord, not from being vindicated before man.

> **Proverbs 12:14** A man shall be satisfied with good by the fruit of *his* mouth: and the recompence of a man's hands shall be rendered unto him.

Why must God be glorified? Only God can save people from sin through Jesus Christ, and God must be glorified so that others will be drawn to Him and see the way of salvation. God's reputation matters. Bringing glory to God matters. What are we willing to sacrifice for God to receive the glory in our situation?

This principle is seen again in the book of John, chapter 9. A man had been blind since birth and the Lord explains that this infirmity will serve a greater purpose.

John 9:3 Jesus answered, Neither hath this man sinned, nor his parents: but that the works of God should be made manifest in him.

Are you facing a challenge to your reputation? Are people talking against you? It is possible that this time of your life is happening so that the works of God can be made clear to others. Let God have the glory. Pray for God to get the glory so that others will be drawn to Him; not for you to get vindication. Let your goal always be to preserve God's reputation. Let your guiding motivation be "Glory to God," not "Glory to me."

Have a Conversation with Your Lord Jesus

  🕊 Lord, in what situations do I feel the need to fight or justify myself out of vindication?

_____
_____

  🕊 Lord, has there been a time when I acted out of self-preservation and got vindication, but you were not glorified?

_____
_____

  🕊 Lord, when I am defending myself against a personal attack, how do I act? In what way does this distract from bringing glory to you?

_____
_____

  🕊 Lord, I want to be motivated by a desire to bring you glory. I want to act in a way to always make you look good so others will be drawn to you.

*Pray...*_____
_____
...listen

CONVERSATION 72

Stay in the Fold

Related Bible Passages			
Old Testament	Psalms	Proverbs	New Testament
Numbers 16	66	13	John 10

Today the Lord beautifully reminded me that I am in His fold. What a great comfort! He is my Great Shepherd and I need his guidance. However, He also showed me that it is my job to remain in the fold. The gate to the fold is open and I can come and go as I please. My Great Shepherd is not going to keep me against my will. He wants a relationship with me when I choose to be in his presence and under his care.

God is wonderful, merciful, powerful, loving, accepting, caring, forgiving and a great shepherd. You can know this doctrinally, but have you experienced it personally?

Psalm 66:5 Come and see the works of God: *he is* terrible *in his* doing toward the children of men.

In order to see, we first have to come to Him. We can't experience Him from a distance. To understand *"his doing toward the children of men,"* we have to be a part of his fold; daily following and relying upon the great shepherd for protection, direction, and fulfillment.

There is no "in-between." We are either in the fold and following the Great Shepherd or we are following another leader. It is a daily decision to stay in the fold and it takes on-purpose focus to stay close to the Lord and follow Him.

> **John 10:11, 14** I am the good shepherd: the good shepherd giveth his life for the sheep. I am the good shepherd, and know my *sheep*, and am known of mine.

Life will get hard and it will seem like the good shepherd is no longer caring and leading. The temptation may become strong to look in a different direction. Our Lord knows that this will happen and warns us that, "The thief cometh not, but for to steal, and to kill, and to destroy: I am come that they might have life, and that they might have *it* more abundantly." (John 10:10)

Many life situations could cause us to look for a different leader: illness, frustration, a lack of productivity, a desire for recognition, a love for entertainment, laziness, and selfishness. All of these and many more situations could cause us to conclude that the good shepherd is no longer interested in leading us and so we entertain the idea of following "thieves." We might become convinced that life away from the great shepherd would be better and safer. Oh, how we can become so deceived! These "thieves" will only kill and destroy. Safety, protection, and love are found only with the great shepherd and in following Him.

The Israelites were in that very situation. They were faced with difficulty and came to the conclusion that they would be better off with another shepherd. In essence, what they were saying was that they no longer wanted to follow and trust, they wanted to lead and take control.

Psalm 66:7 He ruleth by his power for ever; his eyes behold the nations: let not the rebellious exalt themselves. Selah.

The Israelites were rebellious and exalting themselves. They felt they knew better than the Lord. They wanted a captain that would take them where they directed and thus change their circumstances. They wanted to be in charge of their direction.

Numbers 16:2-3 And they rose up before Moses, with certain of the children of Israel, two hundred and fifty princes of the assembly, famous in the congregation, men of renown: And they gathered themselves together against Moses and against Aaron, and said unto them, *Ye take* too much upon you, seeing all the congregation *are* holy, every one of them, and the LORD *is* among them: wherefore then lift ye up yourselves above the congregation of the LORD?

This rebellion was led by Korah and he was the thief. He desired to lead instead of following the Lord and accept his provision, and in this desire, he convinced other Israelites to follow him. He stole them from the flock of God.

The good shepherd will die for you. A thief seeks to destroy you. Following your own way to avoid difficult circumstances or to create your own destiny is following a "thief" and will bring destruction.

"The Lord is my Shepherd" needs to be our declaration. Do you put Him first and allow Him to direct the decisions in your life? When things get difficult will you be tempted to step outside of the fold looking for a new leader?

Proverbs 13:20 He that walketh with wise *men* shall be wise: but a companion of fools shall be destroyed.

Walk with the good shepherd and you will be near his wisdom. If you decide to follow "thieves" you will find yourself surrounded by fools and headed for destruction.

Conversations

Have a Conversation with Your Lord Jesus

🕊 Lord, has there been a time when I tried to leave you looking for another shepherd?

_____
_____

🕊 Lord, when I am tired of waiting for you, do I steal myself away from you to follow after my own direction?

_____
_____

🕊 Lord, when difficulty comes, do I look to find a solution, or do I first try to get closer to you?

_____
_____

🕊 Lord, I know you are good, true, and wise. I know that you love me. Please help me understand why I try to leave your fold. Help me to draw closer to you so that thieves can't steal me away from you.

*Pray...*_____
_____
...listen

Face to Face With Your Lord

CONVERSATION 73

Being a Leader

Related Bible passages			
Old Testament	Psalms	Proverbs	New Testament
Numbers 17	67	14	John 11

In one situation or another, we are leaders. We might not be a leader of a nation, but we might lead our children, or we might lead a group or a project. No matter the nature of our leadership, a good leader must have certain qualities.

During my conversation with the Lord, I had to think about the ways that I am a leader. In some situations, there are people depending on me to step in the right direction. I recognized how careful I must be as I don't want to move others down the wrong path. I need to seek wisdom to ensure that I am making the right decisions. Another part of my conversation with the Lord centered around my motives. Intrinsically I am a people-pleaser. I want to make people happy and I want to make people happy with me. Through this conversation, I saw the selfish nature of this motive and how this motive can taint my ability to make good leadership decisions. If left unchecked, this motive could lead me to make decisions that will bring glory to me rather than glory to God.

The first part of my conversated started with the Lord reminding me that He chooses His leaders. He knows our strengths and weaknesses better than we do. He will place the right leader ahead of us to teach and guide us, and He will give us leadership responsibilities to the extent that we are able to perform them. This is shown in Numbers 17 where the Lord chose Aaron to be a leader.

> **Numbers 17:5** And it shall come to pass, *that* the man's rod, whom I shall choose, shall blossom: and I will make to cease from me the murmurings of the children of Israel, whereby they murmur against you.
>
> **Numbers 17:8** And it came to pass, that on the morrow Moses went into the tabernacle of witness; and, behold, the rod of Aaron for the house of Levi was budded, and brought forth buds, and bloomed blossoms, and yielded almonds.
>
> **Numbers 17:10** And the LORD said unto Moses, Bring Aaron's rod again before the testimony, to be kept for a token against the rebels; and thou shalt quite take away their murmurings from me, that they die not.

The Lord knew that Aaron was the right man to help lead the Israelites. He was put in that position of authority and those under him were expected to willingly submit to his direction and learn from him. The Lord knows us as well. He will choose us to lead, and we are responsible for the direction we lead those we have been given.

Conversations

Leaders are necessary and vital in every area of life but particularly in leading someone's spiritual life. Intrinsically, people truly desire to know the "right" way and we need to be a good leader that will move people in the right direction past the unknown hurdles. In a spiritual sense, we want to be someone who will help draw others closer to the Lord.

Psalm 67:2 That thy way may be known upon earth, thy saving health among all nations.

Who is your leader? Who is trying to keep you on a path that grows you closer to the Lord? Recognizing that leader will help you be sensitive to their direction.

The second part of my conversation with the Lord centered around motive; motive is everything. In order to effectively lead and point people toward the Lord, we have to have a focus on serving the Lord, not gaining the approval of the people. Determining our driving motive can be difficult to identify, but it is critical to making sure that we are being led by the right force, and to make sure we are leading for the right reasons. Why is it dangerous to make winning the approval of others our guiding motive?

Proverbs 14:28 In the multitude of people *is* the king's honour: but in the want of people *is* the destruction of the prince.

If the motive is to gain the approval of others, decisions will be based on meeting this need and not on godly principle. It is a motive to feed pride! The end result is foolish decisions and ultimately leading people in the wrong direction.

In John 11 the Lord explains this beautifully when faced with Lazarus' illness and untimely death.

John 11:4 When Jesus heard *that*, he said, This sickness is not unto death, but for the glory of God, that the Son of God might be glorified thereby.

If the Lord had been motivated by the desire to win the approval of others, He would have run to heal and comfort Mary and Martha. But since He was motivated to bring glory to God, He tarried so that "...the Son of God might be glorified thereby." Mary and Martha were frustrated by his delay, but the end result brought glory to God. This story serves as a great example of how a motive to serve the Lord will direct our decisions, and how people are ultimately served through our motive to bring God glory.

Through this conversation, the Lord clearly showed me that when I get my motives straight, I will quickly realize that through a focus on serving my Lord, the people are served, and needs are met. When I focus on gaining the approval of people, then I end up a failed leader, the people are not served, and the Lord left out of the picture.

You can be a great leader when you recognize your leaders. They are those who have been given to lead you closer to God. They are serving the Lord, rather than themselves, for your benefit. Second, remember that God has given you a position of leadership. Cherish it. He is asking you to lead others down a good path, and toward Him. Keep your motives in check to be sure you are serving God and not trying to gain the approval of man.

Conversations

Have a Conversation with Your Lord Jesus

🕊 Lord, who have you given me to lead?

_____
_____

🕊 Lord, how am I leading them to live righteously, and have a closer spiritual walk with you?

_____
_____

🕊 Lord, when have my motives been to gain the approval of man rather than serving you?

_____
_____

🕊 Lord, I want to be a good leader for you. I want to keep pleasing you as my motivation and lead others in a closer relationship with you. Please help me to be a good leader with the right motives.

Pray...
_____
_____
...listen

Face to Face With Your Lord

Face to Face with Your Lord

CONVERSATION 74

Fishing for the Praise of Men

Related Bible Passages			
Old Testament	Psalms	Proverbs	New Testament
Numbers 20	68	15	John 12

Have you ever been around someone fishing for a compliment? It might seem like they are bragging about their accomplishments or rehashing all they have done for others but what they are really doing is looking for recognition. They may even try criticizing themselves hoping you will contradict them with a compliment. This individual is starving for praise and has come to you fishing for a compliment.

Wanting recognition or a pat on the back for a "job well done" is natural. I have experienced this desire. There is something inside of me that wants to know that I am doing well and headed in the right direction. Even in serving the

Lord I want to hear that I am doing a good job. I desire to hear from other Christians that I am truly making a difference in their lives. But this desire comes with its faults. After reading the passages from my Bible, the Lord had me pause and contemplate the following verse:

> **John 12:43** For they loved the praise of men more than the praise of God.

In the want of praise, I might be drawn to serving people, instead of truly serving the Lord. The praise from people is more tangible and present, but not more fulfilling than the praise that could come from my Lord. If I am serving the Lord, my decisions will be based on pleasing Him. If I am serving people, I will be motivated toward making them happy.

Did Moses struggle with this? It is possible that a desire for recognition motivated him to deviate from the Lord's command. He was constantly receiving the brunt of the Israelites' dissatisfaction. No one thanked him for leading the multitudes. No one thanked him for his wisdom. No one thanked him for his leadership; in fact, this was challenged on numerous occasions. Moses was human and so Moses needed a little encouragement; just a little recognition!

In Numbers 20 the Israelites were dissatisfied, AGAIN!

> **Numbers 20:2** And there was no water for the congregation: and they gathered themselves together against Moses and against Aaron.

You can imagine that these men were tired of being the object of a multitude of complaints. No one recognized how hard they had been working. The Lord told Moses to:

Numbers 20:8 Take the rod, and gather thou the assembly together, thou, and Aaron thy brother, and speak ye unto the rock before their eyes; and it shall give forth his water, and thou shalt bring forth to them water out of the rock: so thou shalt give the congregation and their beasts drink.

When Moses came before the rock with his rod in hand, his flesh might have been overcome with a desire to be recognized for doing something good. He smote the rock with his rod (a physical display to the Israelites of his personal efforts). Water came gushing out of the rock, but Moses had hit the rock with a flare of, "Look at what I am doing for you," instead of quietly speaking to the rock and letting the Lord get the credit for the miracle.

Numbers 20:12 And the LORD spake unto Moses and Aaron, Because ye believed me not, to sanctify me in the eyes of the children of Israel, therefore ye shall not bring this congregation into the land which I have given them.

In the Lord's eyes, He was not honored by Moses' actions. By hitting the rock, Moses brought recognition upon himself. Moses might have been motivated by a desire to get just a little recognition from a hateful group of people, however, it was still an act against what God had commanded.

It is easy to see the rebellious nature of the Israelites. Psalm 68:6 says that "... the rebellious dwell in a dry *land*." How true this is in this story. It even transcends Moses' condition. His decision was born out of a rebellious disposition. It forced him to live in a literal "dry land" for the rest of his life and prevented him from entering the Promised Land.

It takes humility to by-pass the acquisition of human recognition for Godly praise. It takes wisdom and strength to act in such a way where we can harvest praise from the Lord when it is not offered from those around us. Satisfaction comes from knowing you did it the Lord's way and you have His praise.

Proverbs 15:33 The fear of the LORD *is* the instruction of wisdom; and before honour *is* humility.

When we have a healthy fear (reverence) for the Lord, we will desire for Him to get the glory and honor through our actions rather than making sure we are recognized. We will have a humble countenance. Reading in John 12 we come across a very sad situation that is the result of actions motivated by a desire for recognition and praise from man.

John 12:42 Nevertheless among the chief rulers also many believed on him; but because of the Pharisees they did not confess *him*, lest they should be put out of the synagogue:

Many chief rulers believed in Christ, but "because of the Pharisees," they did not confess the Lord. They would not admit that they had believed. Why? These were saved men who were paralyzed in their service toward the Lord because they were so focused on gaining and keeping the praise of men.

John 12:43 For they loved the praise of men more than the praise of God.

Letting your desire for recognition direct your actions can leave you in a "dry land," paralyzed in your service to God. In seeking the approval of man, you will end up unfulfilled. Live and act the way the Lord has directed and be satisfied with his praise. There is nothing more fulfilling than knowing you have pleased Him.

Conversations

Have a Conversation with Your Lord Jesus

☙ Lord, how do I seek praise from others?

_____
_____

☙ Lord, do I love the praise of man more than knowing I have pleased you?

_____
_____

☙ Lord, how does a love of praise from man change my actions and how I feel toward others?

_____
_____

☙ Lord, I want to be motivated by a desire to please you. I want my actions to be what brings you glory. Please help me to be sensitive to a motivation to serve man rather than you.

Pray... _____

_____
...listen

Face to Face With Your Lord

CONVERSATION 75

I Cannot Go Beyond

Related Bible Passages			
Old Testament	Psalms	Proverbs	New Testament
Numbers 22	68	16	John 13

Has the Lord told you to stop and you have decided to go on? Has He set limits in your life and you have decided to go beyond, just a little? Or are there areas in your life where the Lord has opened a door and you just can't quite go through?

In Numbers, I read of a man who verbalized the right perspective in living a controlled life for the Lord but had a difficult time following his own words. I realized that, at times, I have the same problem. The Lord pointed out to me that, in some instances, I have the right words and the right Christian philosophies, but sometimes I have a difficult time displaying them in my own life. This was not an easy conversation to have with my Lord, but needful. There are some areas of my life that I need to get aligned with what I know is right.

Balak was a king of Moab and he had heard of the Israelites and the power of their God. They were conquering people and land. He was worried about his fate and wanted to protect his territory. In order to accomplish this, he wanted the Israelites cursed. Balak sent servants to a man, Balaam, that he knew believed in God and asked him to curse these people.

Balaam had a great answer to this request:

> **Numbers 22:18** And Balaam answered and said unto the servants of Balak, If Balak would give me his house full of silver and gold, I cannot go beyond the word of the LORD my God, to do less or more.

Unfortunately, Balaam did not heed these words of wisdom that flowed from his own mouth.

> **Numbers 22:20-21** And God came unto Balaam at night, and said unto him, If the men come to call thee, rise up, *and* go with them; but yet the word which I shall say unto thee, that shalt thou do. And Balaam rose up in the morning, and saddled his ass, and went with the princes of Moab.

God said, "*If* the men come to call thee...," then Balaam could go with the men. But in the passage, Balaam just rose up in the morning and went! He did not wait to see if the men would come to call him. Balaam did what was right in his own eyes; he did not heed God's words. He went and went beyond what the Lord had commanded with the expectation that God would bless.

> **Proverbs 16:25** There is a way that seemeth right unto a man, but the end thereof *are* the ways of death.

Going with the men seemed right and it was something Balaam wanted to do. It seemed that God gave a conditional allowance, so Balaam took liberty and went. As you read, you will see that Balaam got into trouble for going beyond God's words, and a talking donkey had to get involved!

Now consider a command that the Lord has given us:

John 13:34 A new commandment I give unto you, That ye love one another; as I have loved you, that ye also love one another.

In this verse, God is telling us to love one another. I had to ask myself if I am doing this. Am I loving others in the way Christ has loved me? Am I doing less than this? Am I loving others, or am I only loving those that are easy to love or those that deserve and earn my love? These were not easy questions to discuss with the Lord.

How about you? Consider how you treat others. Consider how you meet the needs of others. How are you showing that you love others?

Verse 35 gives the world permission to judge us by our ability to live out this verse.

John 13:35 By this shall all *men* know that ye are my disciples, if ye have love one to another.

When the world looks at our actions and hears our words, will the world come to the conclusion that we love others?

Has the Lord told you to stop something and you have stepped back into it? Has He told you to stay somewhere and you have decided to step over the line? Metaphorically the Lord drew a line in the sand for Balaam. Balaam sought the Lord's direction, received direction and then chose to go beyond. It is exciting to see the Lord give direction, but in that direction is our responsibility to heed it. When the Lord draws the line, we should not go beyond. When He says go, we should go.

Psalm 68:34 Ascribe ye strength unto God: his excellency *is* over Israel, and his strength *is* in the clouds.

We need to ascribe our strength unto God. Our strength belongs to God and our strength comes from Him. Through His strength, we have the power to heed his direction.

Numbers 22:18 ... I cannot go beyond the word of the LORD my God, to do less or more.

What a great life verse!

Conversations

Have a Conversation with Your Lord Jesus

- Lord, is there something you have told me to do, and I have done less?

  _____
  _____

- Lord, is there something you have told me to stop, and I have gone beyond?

  _____
  _____
  _____

- Lord, do I love others in a way that brings glory and recognition to you?

  _____
  _____

- Lord, I want to live out the verse and not go beyond your word. I want to live out your direction. Please help me recognize your strength in me to follow your directions.

  *Pray...*_____
  _____
  _____*...listen*

CONVERSATION 76

Strive

	Related Bible Passages		
Old Testament	Psalms	Proverbs	New Testament
Numbers 23	69	17	John 15

Have you ever known a person who loves to argue? No matter what you say, they must disagree and contradict your statement. Or there is the person that is critical of every decision you make. They speak out to others about you and criticize your every move, even if it is good. These individuals are given to contention and strife.

Proverbs 17:1 Better *is* a dry morsel, and quietness therewith, than an house full of sacrifices *with* strife.

Proverbs 17:14 The beginning of strife *is as* when one letteth out water: therefore leave off contention, before it be meddled with.

As I read through these verses, I had to pause and consider if I am given to strife. Am I the person who is endlessly critical of others? Do I complain about others? I would hope this would be something that I would not engage in, but I had to admit that there have been times where I found it easy to be critical of others and complain about them to anyone willing to listen.

As it says in Proverbs, causing strife is as easy as letting out water. Water pours easily from any vessel. No effort is needed. The same is true with causing strife through our words. We can strive with a person through argument, or we can cause strife by complaining to others. Finding something to strive over is easy. There is always something to be critical about. There is always someone that is not doing things the way we want or thinking just like us. Are we going to complain; are we going to create strife?

When we decide to strive with someone, the results may be devastating to someone else's heart. The mouth is a very powerful weapon. Some women know how to use that weapon and can bring someone to the point of ultimate misery

> **Psalm 69:2-3** I sink in deep mire, where *there is* no standing: I am come into deep waters, where the floods overflow me. I am weary of my crying: my throat is dried: mine eyes fail while I wait for my God.

The psalmist was experiencing a great degree of misery. He was dealing with the pain of someone striving against him.

> **Psalm 69:12** They that sit in the gate speak against me; and I *was* the song of the drunkards.

> **Psalm 69:14** Deliver me out of the mire, and let me not sink: let me be delivered from them that hate me, and out of the deep waters.

The psalmist knew that he was the topic of conversation amongst his peers. It caused great pain in his life. He could only wish to be delivered from those that hated him.

One of the saddest things I have seen is when a woman brings her husband to this point with her words. She diminishes him to the point at which he feels like he is sinking in the deep mire and wonders what he has done to be so hated.

This woman was given to strife and found it easy to talk out against her husband and others. I know for certain that the Lord did not give her these words!

Numbers 23:12 And he answered and said, Must I not take heed to speak that which the LORD hath put in my mouth?

When you consider a time when you spoke against someone or against your husband, did the Lord give you those words to speak? Did the Lord put words in your mouth for the purpose of bringing someone to the point of utter humiliation and despair? The answer is "No."

There is a stark difference between correcting someone and striving with someone. When our correction is done in love (at our inconvenience and discomfort), it is for the benefit of the other person. When you strive, you are acting out of the sheer joy of diminishing someone and the satisfaction comes to you when he is injured.

The Lord does rebuke people. He admonishes and corrects, but it is done with love and to see the other person be brought closer to Him. When a woman decides to strive with another person, she is not doing it out of love. She is driving the other person to misery and is communicating hatred, not love.

John 15:4 Abide in me, and I in you...

Abide in the Lord. Let Him fill your mouth with the right words to say. Let the Lord use your mouth to draw others to Him. Leave off contention and strife.

Conversations

Have a Conversation with Your Lord Jesus

ಖ Lord, when have I been given to strive with others?

_____
_____

ಖ Lord, am I critical of people for my own gratification?

_____
_____

ಖ Lord, what words have you put in my mouth?

_____
_____

ಖ Lord, you are the governor of my mouth. I want to allow you to control my words and I want to abide close to you.

*Pray...*_____

_____
_____*...listen*

CONVERSATION 77

Zealous

Related Bible Passages			
Old Testament	Psalms	Proverbs	New Testament
Numbers 25	69	18	John 16

What gets you really excited and motivated to get up and go? Are there things that you approach with enthusiasm and intensity? When your focus and attention drive you to passionate action, you are displaying zeal.

This conversation revealed to me that there are some things I need to be zealous about. Zeal is defined as having great energy or enthusiasm in pursuit of a cause or an objective; passion, love, fervor, fire, devotion, enthusiasm, eagerness, keenness, appetite, relish, gusto, vigor, energy, and intensity. So, with that definition in mind, are you zealous for your Lord?

Zealous in Service

Have you ever been in a situation where you knew something had to be done and the Lord told you it was your job to do it? It might have been crazy; without logic, and borderline fanatical, but you were zealous. You did it anyway.

In Numbers 25, driven by a dire situation, Phinehas was zealous for the Lord. There was a situation that needed to be taken care of and he got the job done. He was zealous for his God.

> **Numbers 25:11** Phinehas, the son of Eleazar, the son of Aaron the priest, hath turned my wrath away from the children of Israel, while he was zealous for my sake among them, that I consumed not the children of Israel in my jealousy.

> **Numbers 25:13** ...because he was zealous for his God, and made an atonement for the children of Israel.

Zealous in Praise

Praise the Lord with great energy. Sing a song to Him with love and enthusiasm. Be zealous in your praise. The song service at church is not to be a dry, perfunctory event that is done out of ritual. The song service is not supposed to be a concert that entertains you; its purpose is to provide you with an opportunity to personally and corporately worship God through active participation. Sing! Sing with intensity! Be zealous in praise.

> **Psalm 69:30** I will praise the name of God with a song, and will magnify him with thanksgiving.

Zealous in Relationships

The Lord has given you friends and relationships for the purpose of blessing your life and for you to be a blessing in their life. Be zealous toward your friends.

> **Proverbs 18:24** A man *that hath* friends must shew himself friendly: and there is a friend *that* sticketh closer than a brother.

If you want true friendship, then be zealous; be eager to meet your friend's needs. Be the first-responder to lift her up and encourage her. You will be friendly, interested, and invested in her life. You will be engaged and observant. You will be a friend that will be a benefit to her. The most wonderful thing about being a zealous friend is that it is never a one-way street. The same zeal will be returned to you.

Zealous in Tribulation and Joy

Tribulation will come. Don't crumble and retreat into a dark corner. Be zealous. Press forward through the difficulty with a belief that it will turn to joy. Draw closer to God; do not run from Him. The tribulation you are in will not last forever. Don't despise the tribulation, but rather see it as a vehicle that delivers joy.

> **John 16:20** Verily, verily, I say unto you, That ye shall weep and lament, but the world shall rejoice: and ye shall be sorrowful, but your sorrow shall be turned into joy.

Perhaps the greatest challenge when you are experiencing tribulation, depression, and pain is to make a conscious choice to believe in the promises of God and think on these things rather than being absorbed by your intense emotions.

Conversations

When you are drowning in hopelessness, only a deliberate and zealous faith in God can help you breathe again.

Have a Conversation with Your Lord Jesus

☙ Lord, what am I zealous about; what gets me excited?

_____
_____

☙ Lord, how can I become more zealous for you?

_____
_____

☙ Lord, how does my current zeal form my thoughts, decisions, and actions?

_____
_____
_____

☙ Lord, I want to be zealous about the right things. I want a zeal for you to drive my thoughts and actions.

*Pray...*_____
_____
_____*...listen*

CONVERSATION 78

Speak Up

Related Bible Passages			
Old Testament	Psalms	Proverbs	New Testament
Numbers 27	70	19	John 18

Speak up! It's ok to let people know what you think or what you need. You don't have to sit there in silence waiting for someone to notice that you have something to say or that you have a need. Speak up! It is not wrong, but there is a caveat; it has to be done in the right way. A bad attitude or a harsh tone can mask your words.

Reading through the passages above, I found a message that the Lord was trying to communicate to me. There are some great reasons to speak up and use my voice to deliver something good for my Lord.

Five Sisters Speak Up

Just before the crossing into the promised land five daughters of Zelophehad came before Moses. Their father had died in the wilderness and he had no sons to possess land in their father's name. They spoke up and said:

> **Numbers 27:4** Why should the name of our father be done away from among his family, because he hath no son? Give unto us *therefore* a possession among the brethren of our father.

I am sure this was a bold move on their part. It was not customary for women to come independently before Moses AND make a request to take possession of land among their brethren. Many social barriers had to be overcome for them to find the strength to speak up, but they did. It is important to recognize that they were rewarded for their strength and how they presented their words. They made a clear request.

> **Numbers 27:6-7** And the LORD spake unto Moses, saying, The daughters of Zelophehad speak right: thou shalt surely give them a possession of an inheritance among their father's brethren; and thou shalt cause the inheritance of their father to pass unto them.

David, the Psalmist Speaks Up

We need to speak up before our Lord. He desires to hear us and our requests.

> **Psalm 70:1** *Make haste*, O God, to deliver me; make haste to help me, O LORD.

> **Psalm 70:5** But I *am* poor and needy: make haste unto me, O God: thou *art* my help and my deliverer; O LORD, make no tarrying.

Reading the Psalm, we can hear the intensity of this request. "Make haste...make no tarrying." We can turn to our Lord and come before his throne boldly and speak up. We can let Him know our needs and express our hearts. Not just in times of dire need, but daily.

Peter Speaks Up

It is a dark and scary time for the Lord's disciples. The Lord has been betrayed by Judas and a band of officers has bound Jesus and taken Him to the high priest to be questioned. Peter lurked in the background wanting to know what was going to happen to his Lord, but not wanting to be noticed. Then someone noticed him and asked:

> **John 18:25** ...Art not thou also *one* of his disciples? He denied *it*, and said, I am not.

When the threat of emotional or physical harm is upon us, it becomes easy to speak up and say something out of self-preservation. Peter denied that he knew the Lord to protect himself.

We need to exercise caution when we feel questioned or attacked. Our flesh will want to be protected and we will speak up and say something to defend ourselves. Most of the time, what comes out of our mouth will not be something that honors the Lord. We need to find the strength to speak up in truth even when we feel threatened.

A Wife Speaks Up

You might have heard that to be a good wife you have to be silent; never speaking up or expressing your thoughts. This is not true. Your husband loves you and wants to know your thoughts and dreams and your needs. BUT you have to speak up in the right way! He is not magically gifted with the ability to read your mind. If you believe that he should know what you want without having to say it, you are believing something that will bring you years of disappointment. Speak up!

If it is true that it is good to speak up and that you have something valuable to say, you don't want your words to be lost or masked by tone or decibel level. As women, when we feel frustrated or hurt, we have a way of speaking up that is self-defeating. Our tone becomes harsh, loud, demanding, and disrespectful.

> **Proverbs 19:13** ... the contentions of a wife *are* a continual dropping.

Nagging is defined by tone and frequency, and while nagging might be considered speaking up you will never get your thought communicated. Your words are important, your needs are real, your ideas are enlightening, and your opinions matter. Control your tone and disposition so your words can be heard. Speak up with respect. Speak up with thoughtfulness. Speak up with boldness and truth.

Conversations

Have a Conversation with Your Lord Jesus

ಜ Lord, what needs do I have that I have kept to myself hoping that someone will notice?

_____
_____

ಜ Lord, why am I afraid to speak up?

_____
_____

ಜ Lord, when do I lose control of my tone and let it mask my words?

_____
_____

ಜ Lord, I know you give me wisdom and I know you give me good direction. Help me to speak up at the right moment, with thoughtful words and with a tone that helps me communicate what you have given me.

Pray... _____
_____
...listen

Face to Face With Your Lord

CONVERSATION 79

Stay Close

Related Bible Passages			
Old Testament	Psalms	Proverbs	New Testament
Numbers 30	71	20	John 19

It is true that the Lord will never leave you nor forsake you but that does not mean that "nearness" is automatic. You have to work daily on maintaining that relationship with the Lord. He will never leave you, but you do have the potential to wander, get distracted, or even walk away. You have to make an effort to stay close; daily, hourly, every minute realigning your spirit and drawing near to Him.

As the idea of staying close to my Lord was forming in my mind, the Lord brought to mind my daughter and my nearness to her. By being close to her I have a window into her personality. I can see her strengths and weaknesses and through this knowledge, I know what will cause her harm and how to protect her. As a young child, she did not have that degree of wisdom to protect herself. As an adult, I had to intervene for her to thrive. A child will not thrive if left alone. In Numbers, the Lord showed me that a father that is near can disallow a daughter's errant vow. He can intervene to ensure her safety and protect her emotionally and physically. If he was not close to hear her words or know her thoughts, he would not know how to guide his daughter.

> **Numbers 30:5** But if her father disallow her in the day that he heareth; not any of her vows, or of her bonds wherewith she hath bound her soul, shall stand: and the LORD shall forgive her, because her father disallowed her.

The Lord continued to show me that as a child of God, I need the same protection. I have to be close to my Lord to hear His direction. I have to acknowledge that I do not have all wisdom inside of me and that I am not wise to all the dangers around me. There is much I do not know and much I do not understand. But my God knows me and He can guide me and intervene in my best interest. He knows how to protect me. I NEED a father that is near. I need to keep myself close to God.

Have you ever had a time that you wandered away from God and forgot that you need to stay close? When this happens, it is because you have become deceived and believed that you can "see all things." It is at this moment that you skitter ignorantly away from your God. Without prayer and wise counsel, you step forward. The distance between you and your source of wisdom gapes wide open.

Proverbs 20:20 warns us that, "Whoso curseth his father or his mother, his lamp shall be put out in obscure darkness." This is where we will find ourselves when we don't stay close to God. If we trust in our ability to "figure it out" and leave

Conversations

God out of the picture, we are at great risk of ending up in obscure darkness.

We can't live this life without our Father. We must have His wisdom and direction and so we must do our job to stay close. Start the day with the proclamation, "In thee, O LORD, do I put my trust: let me never be put to confusion." (Psalm 71:1)

Wandering away from Jesus can lead to our confusion and stress but being near to Jesus can also be uncomfortable. The closer you get to Jesus the more you will start to see how magnificent the Lord truly is, and how much grace He has actually extended to you because of your sinful nature. There is an immeasurable difference between a holy God and sinful man; but yet He makes a way where you can still get close and have a friendly relationship with the creator of this universe.

Mary, the mother of Jesus stayed close to Him even in a confusing and terrifying moment.

> **John 19:25** Now there stood by the cross of Jesus his mother, and his mother's sister, Mary the *wife* of Cleophas, and Mary Magdalene.

She stayed close to Jesus beholding her son's suffering. I am sure that she desired with every thread of her being that she could rescue Him from this suffering, but in his suffering, He provided for her needs. She was near, she stayed close, and even in the midst of His suffering the Lord Jesus cared for His mother and directed one of His disciples to care for her and comfort her. She was near to Him and He took care of her.

> **John 19:26-27** When Jesus therefore saw his mother, and the disciple standing by, whom he loved, he saith unto his mother, Woman, behold thy son! Then saith

he to the disciple, Behold thy mother! And from that hour that disciple took her unto his own *home*.

He can do the same for you. Stay close to the Lord. Here you will feel and know his amazing love, care, guidance, and protection.

Conversations

Have a Conversation with Your Lord Jesus

☒ Lord, when have I wandered away from you?

_____
_____

☒ Lord, what do I need to do to stay close to you?

_____
_____

☒ Lord, when I have been close, how have you provided for me?

_____
_____

☒ Lord, I want to stay close to you to have your wisdom, direction, and protection. I want to keep my focus on you.

*Pray...*_____

_____
_____*...listen*

Face to Face With Your Lord

CONVERSATION 80

Lovest Thou Me

Related Bible Passages

Old Testament	Psalms	Proverbs	New Testament
Numbers 31	71:14-24	21	John 21

The Israelites were attacking and moving out the tribes that stood in their way of possessing their land. These groups opposed the Israelites and stood in their way physically and spiritually.

> **Numbers 31:7-8** And they warred against the Midianites, as the LORD commanded Moses; and they slew all the males. And they slew the kings of Midian, beside the rest of them that were slain; *namely,* Evi, and Rekem, and Zur, and Hur, and Reba, five kings of Midian: Balaam also the son of Beor they slew with the sword.

<u>Balaam is among the dead!</u> Why?! Wasn't he one of the good guys? We read in "Conversation 75" that he refused to

curse the children of Israel. He was the one that said "...I cannot go beyond the word of the LORD my God, to do less or more." (Numbers 22:18) Why is he numbered with the dead of Midian?

Back in Numbers 25 and in "Conversation 77" we read about how the Israelites were committing sin with the women of Midian. Phinehas was zealous for his Lord and put an end to the idolatry and fornication. According to Numbers 31, this idolatry and fornication were at the counsel of Balaam. He put this temptation before the children of Israel!

> **Numbers 31:16** Behold, these caused the children of Israel, through the counsel of Balaam, to commit trespass against the LORD in the matter of Peor, and there was a plague among the congregation of the LORD.

Amazing. I guess since he could not curse the children of Israel, he found a way to get them to curse themselves by putting temptation before their eyes. Look at what Revelation 2:14 has to say about Balaam:

> **Revelation 2:14** But I have a few things against thee, because thou hast there them that hold the doctrine of Balaam, who taught Balac to cast a stumblingblock before the children of Israel, to eat things sacrificed unto idols, and to commit fornication.

Why did Balaam do this to the children of Israel? 2 Peter 2:15 says that Balaam "...loved the wages of unrighteousness..." Balaam was not committed to the Lord and the Lord's ways. He was committed to setting his own course of acquiring power, recognition, and comfort. He figured he had found a "loophole" in God's commands so that he could get what he wanted. There are no loopholes in God's word nor are there any ways to get around His commandments.

Conversations

Proverbs 21:16 The man that wandereth out of the way of understanding shall remain in the congregation of the dead.

Balaam had an understanding of the power of God but was not committed to God's ways. Balaam was committed to his own advancement, securing his own comfort, and setting his own course. He was lusting after self-promotion and was willing to leave God behind in order to achieve gratification.

Psalms 71 reminds us that God will increase our greatness and will take care of our comfort; it is not something we have to contrive.

Psalm 71:21 Thou shalt increase my greatness, and comfort me on every side.

God will take care of promoting you. You do not need to force a situation to make sure you are recognized. God will take care of your comfort; you do not need to turn your back on God's direction to obtain comfort and security.

It really all comes down to deciding what you love. Do you love the Lord enough to trust Him? I wonder what Balaam would have said if the Lord had asked him the same question He asked Peter?

John 21:15 So when they had dined, Jesus saith to Simon Peter, Simon, *son* of Jonas, lovest thou me more than these? He saith unto him, Yea, Lord; thou knowest that I love thee. He saith unto him, Feed my lambs.

I think I know that answer. Balaam loved the "wages of unrighteousness" more than the Lord. He loved promoting himself and contriving his own recognition, comfort, and promotion rather than letting the Lord build it for him. As I concluded this conversation with the Lord, I had to consider what do I love more than the Lord? Is it comfort, promotion, or recognition? When am I willing to set aside a right heart and a right spirit so that I can think or do what I want?

How about you? What do you love more than the Lord? In what situation are you willing to set aside your relationship with the Lord so you can do or take what you want?

Set your heart, spirit, and thoughts so that they are committed on the Lord. Peter said to the Lord:

> **John 21:17** ...Lord, thou knowest all things; thou knowest that I love thee...

These words can be easy to say, but are they evidenced by the things you do? What does the Lord see as evidence of your love, or does He see another Balaam?

Conversations

Have a Conversation with Your Lord Jesus

🕊 Lord, what do I love more than you?

_____
_____

🕊 Lord, when have I set aside my relationship with you so that I could do or think about what I wanted?

_____
_____

🕊 Lord, do you know that I love you? How do I show it?

_____
_____

🕊 Lord, "...thou knowest all things; thou knowest that I love thee..." Help me to remember my love for you and not leave you behind to seek my own lusts.

Pray...
_____
_____
...listen

Face to Face With Your Lord

CONVERSATION 81

Take Time for Change

Related Bible Passages			
Old Testament	Psalms	Proverbs	New Testament
Numbers 33	72	22	Acts 1

The other day I saw a website that encouraged people to change their ways and make their lives better with the Lord's help. The website said that all you have to do is to pray this simple prayer, "Lord Jesus change my _____". All you had to do was fill in the blank and pray that prayer. Then you sit back and watch the Lord work!

Shortly after I saw that website, the Lord had me read the above passages. He reminded me that change is a process that requires effort and attention on my part. It is not a magic trick that the Lord performs and I get to sit back a watch. I had to wonder if there were areas in my life where I am expecting the Lord to make a change but I was putting forth no effort to ensure that it happen.

Through these passages, the Lord showed me that He is not obligated to act when I say some magic words. It does not work that way. Change takes time, a relationship with the Lord, and WORK. Change does not come by repeating some set of words and believing that my words will somehow unlock God's power in my life.

You know this in principle, but are you guilty of expecting God to act with no effort on your part? Lord, please grow our church - yet you don't invite anyone. Lord, please help my marriage - yet you don't change how you treat your husband. Lord, please _____ - yet you make no effort to make the change.

If you want to make a change, it takes time:

It took the Israelites 40 years to get from Egypt to the promised land. They were not instantly teleported to the place that God wanted them. It took time. You can read of their long journey in Numbers 33. They left Egypt with a superficial knowledge of their God and 40 years later through trials and training, that organism of people was spiritually transformed. The Israelites needed to change their physical location, but they also needed to heal and change their spiritual condition. It took this group 40 years before they were finally ready to trust the Lord. Even after their arrival, they still had work they had to do to protect their spiritual condition.

> **Numbers 33:55** But if ye will not drive out the inhabitants of the land from before you; then it shall come to pass, that those which ye let remain of them *shall be* pricks in your eyes, and thorns in your sides, and shall vex you in the land wherein ye dwell.

God was not going to do this automatically for them. The Israelites had to take charge of protecting their land and put forth the effort to push out evil influences. They had to build a relationship with the Lord, and they had to work to get to the place that God wanted them. Change takes time. If you are needing to make a change to your spirit, give it time and give it constant attention.

If you want to make a change, it takes a relationship:

> **Psalm 72:18** Blessed *be* the LORD God, the God of Israel, who only doeth wondrous things.

How do you know that God does wondrous things? How do you know that you can trust Him? How do you know that He is faithful? It only comes through having experienced the Lord. The only way you can trust His timing is because you have a relationship with Him and you have seen Him work. Draw close to Him. Read your Bible. Listen. Talk to God. A change in your life will not happen without a relationship with God.

If you want to make a change, it takes WORK:

> **Proverbs 22:6** Train up a child in the way he should go: and when he is old, he will not depart from it.

Does a child instantly know how to act and react? No, it takes 18+ years of molding and making a child into a responsible adult. It takes training; it takes work. We do not expect a child to be born mature, so we should not expect our spiritual life to be instantly mature without training and work.

Even the disciples needed a little nudge to get to work.

> **Acts 1:10-11** And while they looked stedfastly toward heaven as he went up, behold, two men stood by

them in white apparel; Which also said, Ye men of Galilee, why stand ye gazing up into heaven? this same Jesus, which is taken up from you into heaven, shall so come in like manner as ye have seen him go into heaven.

Why are you just standing there? You have work to do. Get busy! The disciples stood there waiting for something to happen, but the Lord Jesus had given them a job to do.

Acts 1:8 But ye shall receive power, after that the Holy Ghost is come upon you: and ye shall be witnesses unto me both in Jerusalem, and in all Judaea, and in Samaria, and unto the uttermost part of the earth.

It was time for them to get busy doing what God had given them to do. "Work" is not a bad word, yet many people avoid it like the plague. As a society, we want to place our order and have it delivered. God does not operate that way. We can make our request to Him, but then we have to engage. With God's help, we have to build a relationship with our Lord, give it time to develop, and be ready to do the necessary work.

Conversations

Have a Conversation with Your Lord Jesus

☙ Lord, what have I asked you to change in my life?

_____
_____

☙ Lord, in what areas of my life am I expecting you to make the change for me?

_____
_____

☙ Lord, what changes do you want me to make?

_____
_____

☙ Lord, if there is work that needs to be done to make the change, then I will do it. Help me to see what I can do, draw closer to you for the strength, and give it time for the change to take place.

*Pray...*_____
_____
_____*...listen*

Face to Face With Your Lord

Face to Face with Your Lord

CONVERSATION 82

Desire, Vengeance, and Envy

Related Bible Passages			
Old Testament	Psalms	Proverbs	New Testament
Numbers 35	73	23	Acts 2

What are you thinking about? It is a fact that you can think about only one thing at a time. Your brain cannot multitask. In addition, your thoughts form the pathway for real action and your thoughts conjure up real emotions.

Proverbs 23:7 For as he thinketh in his heart, so *is* he...

This verse is a reminder that our thoughts will form our personality and demeanor. We need to be very careful with what we let ourselves think about.

We might be under the impression that our thoughts are unknown to others. Largely, this might be true, but not to the degree that we assume. Our thoughts have a way of seeping into our behavior and actions. This could be good or bad. It depends on what we allow ourselves to think on.

As I considered these verses, the Lord brought back a memory of a book that I had read to my children. I can't remember the title, but the main character was a little girl who was unhappy about her current living situation. Her two brothers were driving her crazy. She hatched a plan to run away and live in a museum. The book said that she had thought so much about running away, that when it came time for her to actually take the steps, it was easy. She had run away so many times in her thoughts that the actual action was not hard.

The same is true for us. What we allow ourselves to think on creates a path for us to act. If we allow our thoughts to be consumed with desire, vengeance, or envy these thoughts will eventually corrupt our emotions and actions.

What are you thinking about?

Desire

Is there something you deeply desire? Do you have an appetite for love, affection, attraction, or recognition? Your thoughts could be circling around the intrigue of acquiring these things and you will find yourself drawn to taking them. Maybe even devising a plan to take what you want. A thought life focused on "If only...," I wish...," or "I want..." will turn you into a very dissatisfied and discontent person.

> **Proverbs 23:1-3** When thou sittest to eat with a ruler, consider diligently what *is* before thee: And put a knife to thy throat, if thou *be* a man given to appe-

tite. Be not desirous of his dainties: for they *are* deceitful meat.

A thought life focused on desire will lead you down a path of deceit.

Envy

As you observe even the foolish and mean-spirited people around you it is not hard to recognize that sometimes they appear to have great peace and live lives without want. They continue to mock God and yet their life gets better and better.

> **Psalm 73:3-5** For I was envious at the foolish, *when* I saw the prosperity of the wicked. For *there are* no bands in their death: but their strength *is* firm. They *are* not in trouble *as other* men; neither are they plagued like *other* men.

How can this be? Your thoughts might question God and why He seems to not let you get away with anything but, yet these people appear to be getting away with murder.

Envious thoughts will lead you to question the consistency of God. You will start to wonder how God can treat someone one way and you another. This thought life will lead you to a scary place which is to believe in a God that you cannot trust.

Vengeance

Has someone hurt you? Said something that offended you? If so, your thoughts could be centered on punishing that person for hurting you; that person has to pay in some way.

The Lord had to create cities of refuge to protect people from a vengeful spirit. If a man killed another man accidentally, he could run to a City of Refuge to escape men that might want vengeance.

Many times, when someone has hurt you, it was an accident. They had a different motive, but your heart saw it as an attack. Now you want vengeance.

> **Numbers 35:11-12** Then ye shall appoint you cities to be cities of refuge for you; that the slayer may flee thither, which killeth any person at unawares. And they shall be unto you cities for refuge from the avenger; that the manslayer die not, until he stand before the congregation in judgment.

Are your thoughts filled with a vengeance against another person? Your storm of thoughts will be about scenes where this other person is humiliated and reduced to something morally beneath you. These thoughts will not be hidden, and your destructive attitude will be evident to everyone.

Truth

Take control of your thoughts. Take heed of YOUR spirit. Focus your thoughts on truth. Don't spend excessive think time trying to figure out someone else's spirit or motives. Don't waste time wondering why you don't see God correcting their life. Train your thoughts to be about YOUR condition before God. If you focus your thoughts on truth, you will be filled with wisdom, understanding, direction, and comfort that can only come from the Lord Jesus.

> **Acts 2:28** Thou hast made known to me the ways of life; thou shalt make me full of joy with thy countenance.

Conversations

Have a Conversation with Your Lord Jesus

📖 Lord, what or who are my thoughts focused on?

_____

_____

📖 Lord, what actions will my thoughts lead me to do?

_____

_____

📖 Lord, has there ever been a time where I took control of my thoughts and changed them?

_____

_____

📖 Lord, I want to think about things that are true, and I want my thoughts to lead me to do good things for you.

Pray... _____

_____
_____*...listen*

Face to Face With Your Lord

CONVERSATION 83

I'm Just Talking

Related Bible Passages			
Old Testament	Psalms	Proverbs	New Testament
Deuteronomy 1	73	24	Acts 3

When you are with your close friend you might feel the freedom to vent. You know no one else is around. No one will be hurt, so you feel safe to speak your mind. You might take this opportunity to murmur or complain about others. You justify your words by saying "I am just venting," or "I am just talking," but those words mean things and they will have an effect on you and on others.

The Lord showed me today that never are words, just words. Words that I let leave my mouth, even when I am just venting, will have an effect on me and on everyone that hears me. My words are also heard by my Lord. My words never vanish as if they were never said.

Deuteronomy 1:27 And ye murmured in your tents, and said, Because the LORD hated us, he hath brought us forth out of the land of Egypt, to deliver us into the hand of the Amorites, to destroy us.

Deuteronomy 1:34-35 And the LORD heard the voice of your words, and was wroth, and sware, saying, Surely there shall not one of these men of this evil generation see that good land, which I sware to give unto your fathers,

The Lord hears your words, even when you are in the privacy of your "tent" talking with your family or venting to your friends. Whatever you are complaining about (your church family, your pastor, your husband, your co-workers, etc.) you are, in essence, complaining about God's provision and His ability to intervene. He knows when you are not trusting Him, and as you can see in Deuteronomy, God does not take this lightly.

Complaining and venting come so naturally! Why is this so?

Psalm 73:22 So foolish *was* I, and ignorant: I was *as* a beast before thee.

Proverbs 24:9 The thought of foolishness *is* sin: and the scorner *is* an abomination to men.

When we murmur and complain we reveal our foolishness and lack of understanding of the Lord's ways. We show that we do not trust in the Lord. This is revealed to you, your Lord, and those to which you vent and complain. Complaining is so much easier than trusting. So, how do we turn a murmuring attitude into a trusting and joyful attitude?

Psalm 73:28 But *it is* good for me to draw near to God: I have put my trust in the Lord GOD, that I may declare all thy works.

Draw near to God. Put your trust in Him. Declare all His wonderful works. If your mouth is busy talking about how wonderful your God is, it won't have time to murmur. Typically, when you want to complain about the works of men (and women), you will do it in your "tent" and possibly secretively with a friend, or your family members. When you want to declare the goodness of God, you will come out of your tent and tell the world.

Take the example of the lame man healed by Jesus:

Acts 3:8 And he leaping up stood, and walked, and entered with them into the temple, walking, and leaping, and praising God.

There is a significant difference between sitting in private, murmuring against men and leaping in front of others declaring the goodness of God. Recognizing that your words have an effect on you and those around you, can you imagine the profound effect that leaping and praising God would have on your disposition opposed to sitting in your "tent" murmuring? The effect on your perspective would be transforming!

Have a Conversation with Your Lord Jesus

☙ Lord, have I fallen into a pattern of complaining?

_____
_____

☙ Lord, what things do I typically vent and complain about?

_____
_____

☙ Lord, how do my words reveal that I am not trusting in you?

_____
_____

☙ Lord, I want to use my words to tell others how wonderful you are and not waste time complaining. Help me to have the words to say.

*Pray...*_____
_____
_____*...listen*

CONVERSATION 84

Life Sentence

Related Bible Passages			
Old Testament	Psalms	Proverbs	New Testament
Deuteronomy 3	74	25	Acts 4

Have you ever been handed a life sentence? Probably not one where you were sent to jail for the rest of your life for a heinous crime. But the Bible speaks of a horrible life sentence in a spiritual sense that has been passed to all man. The crime is sin and the judgment is eternal separation from God. No one can enter the glory of Heaven still needing to pay the price for her sin.

As I read through the verses above, the Lord caused me to remember when I was serving a life sentence. Every wrong deed, every selfish motive, every white lie created a debt that I owed to God. He is holy and I was not. Unfortunately, this debt created by sin was not something that I could clear myself. There was no way for me to remove or pay off this debt.

Not even good works could remove the debt created by my sin. Since God loves me, he provided a way for this debt to be removed.

The only way to clear the debt was to allow someone else to pay it for me; someone that lived without sin and was willing to die to pay the debt. "For the wages of sin *is* death; but the gift of God *is* eternal life through Jesus Christ our Lord." (Romans 6:23) This is why God came in the form of Jesus Christ so that His perfect life, death, and resurrection could make a way for my debt to be forgiven.

> **Acts 4:12** Neither is there salvation in any other: for there is none other name under heaven given among men, whereby we must be saved.

Jesus Christ was willing to pay my sin debt on my behalf. Because of Jesus Christ, I could be saved from serving my life sentence. I didn't have to serve my sentence of being separated from God! How could I pass on an offer like that? The forgiveness offered by Jesus Christ released me from my life sentence. When Jesus (who is God) died on the cross, he paid off my sin debt and released me from my life sentence. But this was a gift that I had to be willing to receive; it did not happen automatically. I had to pray and tell the Lord that I knew I was a sinner deserving of a life sentence of Hell and that I would like to receive the gift of forgiveness provided through Jesus Christ. This required faith. I can tell you that He saved me from my life sentence. I am so glad that I took the gift that He offered.

Have you ever received His gift; have you been released from your life sentence? If not, Jesus Christ is ready with a gift of salvation for you too!

Regrettably, even after we receive the gift of forgiveness offered through Jesus Christ, there will still be times in our

Conversations

lives where we will do something willfully wrong against God. We are forever forgiven and our home in heaven is secure, but we will still make bad decisions. We know that God would not let us get away with it, so we brace ourselves for the judgment, but nothing happens. In contrast, sometimes we will do something wrong and the punishment is swift but temporary. But sometimes, if we willfully make a sinful decision that is against God, we will find ourselves faced with a permanent, life-long, unending consequences.

Consider the sin of Adam and Eve. They ate of the tree of knowledge of good and evil, and the consequences were permanent. They were sentenced to a life outside of the garden. If they had asked God, "Can we please return to the garden. We are really sorry." God's answer would have been are resounding "NO."

Moses' sin also had permanent consequences. Still desiring to step foot on the promised land, Moses had hope that God would show him some mercy and shorten his sentence, but his sentence was a permanent consequence of his sin.

> **Deuteronomy 3:24-26** O Lord GOD, thou hast begun to shew thy servant thy greatness, and thy mighty hand: for what God *is there* in heaven or in earth, that can do according to thy works, and according to thy might? I pray thee, let me go over, and see the good land that *is* beyond Jordan, that goodly mountain, and Lebanon. But the LORD was wroth with me for your sakes, and would not hear me: and the LORD said unto me, Let it suffice thee; speak no more unto me of this matter.

Moses desired mercy, and God said NO. God is not obligated to show us mercy and remove the consequence of our sin. He will, however, be with us and guide us to a greater relationship with Him while serving a life sentence resulting from our sin.

The enduring punishment of sin might lead one to believe that she has been abandoned by God. She might cry out,

> **Psalm 74:1** O God, why hast thou cast *us* off for ever? *why* doth thine anger smoke against the sheep of thy pasture?

But God is present in the consequences; He is intimately a part of the consequences that come as a result of willful sin. He is near even though she is suffering the consequences.

Do you feel like you are living through a season of punishment? Living through the period of judgment (even if it is a life sentence) can be a desperate and lonely time, but you have to remember that God is still with you. Don't run from Him because He is punishing you. Don't despise His correction. His love for you does not end even if the consequence lasts a lifetime.

Enduring the consequences of sin can be miserable, and discouragement might pull you back to that original sin. Rule your decisions so you stay close to the Lord. Align your life to act differently. Let the correction change your ways so that you don't fall back into the same sin. Rule your own spirit; don't be ruled by temptation and sin.

> **Proverbs 25:28** He that *hath* no rule over his own spirit *is like* a city *that is* broken down, *and* without walls.

Conversations

Have a Conversation with Your Lord Jesus

☙ Lord, am I serving a life sentence?

_____
_____

☙ Lord, have I pushed you away because you correct me when I sin?

_____
_____

☙ Lord, how am I ruling my own spirit so that I stay away from sin?

_____
_____

☙ Lord, I want to serve a life sentence of being close to you. Thank you for loving me enough to correct me and for being near to comfort me.

*Pray...*_____
_____
_____*...listen*

Face to Face With Your Lord

CONVERSATION 85

Memory

Related Bible Passages			
Old Testament	Psalms	Proverbs	New Testament
Deuteronomy 4	74	26	Acts 5

When you have a moment to just sit back and let your mind wander, what do you think about? What things do you remember?

Sitting in a moment of quietness I thought back to my childhood and running with my friends. I remember times with my family. I even have some memories of my grandfather that were formed when I was very young. I remember major life events and the emotions that came with them like when I got married and when I had my children. It is good to take a moment to remember the things of the past.

It is in those quiet times, God has something He wants us to remember.

> **Deuteronomy 4:9** Only take heed to thyself, and keep thy soul diligently, lest thou forget the things which thine eyes have seen, and lest they depart from thy heart all the days of thy life: but teach them thy sons, and thy sons' sons;

God knows the limitations of my human mind and knows that if I don't take time to remember I will forget. There are many times that my mother asks me if I remember a particular event in my childhood. Many times I have to say I have no memory. It has been lost.

In the same way, we have the potential to forget how great God has been in our lives and how He has blessed us and guided us. In order to prevent this memory loss, we should daily, take a moment to remember our God. Remember God's great acts in history and in our lives. Remember His promises. Take time to remember when we have wandered in the past, as it will help keep us on the right path today. Rehearsing our past and how God has shown himself faithful will give us the strength to face the next day and be reminded that God is with us.

> **Psalm 74:12-13** For God *is* my King of old, working salvation in the midst of the earth. Thou didst divide the sea by thy strength: thou brakest the heads of the dragons in the waters.

God has shown himself to be powerful and faithful in your life. He revealed himself in a certain way to the Israelites, and while God may not have parted the Red Sea for you, He has revealed himself in special ways to you. In Deuteronomy 4:35 Moses said to the Israelites, "Unto thee it was shewed..." God was faithful to show the Israelites that He was present in their lives and He has done the same thing for you. Look back, remember, and remind yourself of God's great presence in your life.

Memory also serves to keep us from repeating the past. Remembering when we have made bad decisions can be uncomfortable, but it should serve only one purpose; to keep us from making the same mistake twice.

Proverbs 26:11 As a dog returneth to his vomit, *so* a fool returneth to his folly.

A fool will make the same bad decision repeatedly because the memory of the consequences has faded. We should not make the same mistake. Take time to remember those times where you have turned your back on God and went your own way, or that time you ignored Him for a season. Remember the consequences and how your decision hurt you or others. Then use that memory to not return to that same pattern of living.

When we don't take time to remember God and His works, then we will forget the blessings that we have witnessed, and our hearts will suffer the loss of having no memory of God's goodness. This is why it is so important to spend some portion of each day to remember what God has done for us. Write down blessings, His correction, and direction and then we should look back in that journal and review all that He has done for us.

The last part of Deuteronomy 4:9 encourages you to tell your children and grandchildren of all the things that the Lord has done for you. This is a natural outcome to contemplating and remembering your great God. You will be compelled to share what you remember.

Deuteronomy 4:9 ...but teach them thy sons, and thy sons' sons;

Acts 5:20 Go, stand and speak in the temple to the people all the words of this life.

Acts 5:42 And daily in the temple, and in every house, they ceased not to teach and preach Jesus Christ.

Sharing what God has done in your life is another great way to remember all His works. Share it with your friends, but most importantly share it with your family. When you experience a blessing from the Lord, the blessing is largely missed by your family unless you tell them about it. Tell your children about what God did for you today. Help them develop eyes to see God's hand through your experiences.

Daily, remember the great things your Lord has done for you and daily pass those experiences on to others. Feed your faith with the memory of God's goodness, and then share what you remember with others.

Conversations

Have a Conversation with Your Lord Jesus

☙ Lord, what blessings did I observe today?

_____
_____

☙ Lord, did I tell anyone about what you have done for me? Who should I tell?

_____
_____

☙ Lord, what can I remember about how you have worked in my life?

_____
_____

☙ Lord, I want to remember, and I want to share. You have been so good to me and I am amazed that you would lead, guide, and inspire me as you continue to tenderly lead on. I love the opportunity to talk about you with others.

*Pray...*_____
_____
                                        ...listen

Face to Face With Your Lord

CONVERSATION 86

The Mom Speech

Related Bible Passages			
Old Testament	Psalms	Proverbs	New Testament
Deuteronomy 5	75	27	Acts 6

"Now be good, do as you are told, listen to God, be friendly to others, and make sure you say 'please', and be thankful. Be a blessing to others and have a good time but be smart." Every time I sent my kids off, some version of this speech went with them. The words might have varied, but the gist was the same - Remember what you have been taught!

The "mom speech" is a quick summary of everything a mom wants her kids to remember when they are stepping outside of her reach of influence for a short period of time. As a mom, I wanted to give them some quick words that would live in their short-term memory of what I expected from them. It was a quick reminder of what was important. I would then send them off knowing that ultimately, they would make their own decisions. I would pray that my training would influence their decisions; I hoped they would bring a smile to my face and bring glory to God.

As I read through today's passages, I recognized the mom speech in many verses. In Acts 6, the apostles are having difficulty meeting the requirements of the ministry as well as meeting the physical needs of the congregation. They decided to find seven men who would assist the apostles with serving the people. Then the apostles could focus on delivering the word of the Lord. Once these men were chosen, they were given clear direction and a blessing to go forward and serve.

> **Acts 6:6** Whom they set before the apostles: and when they had prayed, they laid *their* hands on them.

This is the essence of the mom-speech. Before I sent your children off, I would lay my hands on them, tell them that I love them and remind them of their responsibilities.

Moses was giving the Israelites a very similar speech in Deuteronomy 5 and 6. His "children" were about to depart from his eyesight and from his realm of influence. He was sending them off with some final words.

> **Deuteronomy 5:31-33** But as for thee, stand thou here by me, and I will speak unto thee all the commandments, and the statutes, and the judgments, which thou shalt teach them, that they may do *them* in the land which I give them to possess it. Ye shall observe to do therefore as the LORD your God hath commanded you: ye shall not turn aside to the right hand or to the left. Ye shall walk in all the ways which the LORD your God hath commanded you, that ye may live, and *that it may be* well with you, and *that* ye may prolong *your* days in the land which ye shall possess.

Conversations

"Remember, you are God's children. Be good, do as you have been told, listen to God, be good to others, be thankful, enjoy the new land but be careful..." Why did Moses take the time to tell the children of Israel what they probably already knew? Certainly, they had heard these words before; Moses was not giving them any new revelation or adding to the 10 commandments. Why was he compelled to give this speech as he sent off those he loved?

A mom wants to remind her children that they don't get to act out every impulse. They don't get to let that sin nature rule. The "mom speech" reminds her children that they have to control themselves.

> **Psalm 75:4-5** I said unto the fools, Deal not foolishly: and to the wicked, Lift not up the horn: Lift not up your horn on high: speak *not with* a stiff neck.

Every child has a vein of foolishness and wickedness. The "mom speech" is a reminder to fight that nature. "Think before you speak; think before you act."

A mom also wants to remind her children that they represent their family. Their actions will give the family a good name or a tarnished name.

> **Proverbs 27:11** My son, be wise, and make my heart glad, that I may answer him that reproacheth me.

If a mom will lovingly and carefully give the "mom speech" to her children, and Moses will send the children of God away with a speech of guidance, I find it easy to believe that my God would do the same for me every day. As you sit reading your Bible every morning, can you find where your Lord is giving you words of encouragement for the day? Envision the Lord resting His hands upon you and tenderly saying, "I love you. Have a good day, be nice to others, and be thankful. Remember to stay away from sin and don't act foolishly. Be a blessing to me. Bring a smile to my face today. Remember, I love you."

As you read through your Bible each day look for these messages; look for the mom-speech that the Lord is giving you. Each day He has special words just for you as you face your day.

Conversations

Have a Conversation with Your Lord Jesus

❧ Lord, what words of guidance do you have for me today?

_____
_____

❧ Lord, have there been times that I forgot your direction and acted on impulse?

_____
_____

❧ Lord, when was a time that I received your direction for the day and let it guide my decisions?

_____
_____

❧ Lord, I know you are guiding me. When I go out today, I want to bring a smile to your face.

*Pray...*_____

_____
_____*...listen*

Face to Face With Your Lord

CONVERSATION 87

Decide Now

Related Bible Passages			
Old Testament	Psalms	Proverbs	New Testament
Deuteronomy 7	76	28	Acts 7

Reading through these passages, the Lord convinced me that I need to set limits on how I will act in any given situation. If I don't, my reactions to stressful situations will be ungoverned. This could be dangerous! I want to know how I will act and have a plan set so that when the time comes, I have something that will rule my actions and reactions.

What limits have you set on your actions and reactions? Have you set a personal standard of behavior that rules how you will act in a stressful or challenging situation? If you do have not set a standard that governs your actions, distress will dictate how you respond.

If you don't set a personal standard of behavior, emotions will rule.

Proverbs 28:26 He that trusteth in his own heart is a fool: but whoso walketh wisely, he shall be delivered.

The heart is deceitful, and to base our response to a situation based on how we feel is dangerous. It is possible that we may not be "feeling" the right thing in a given situation. Why can't we trust our heart or, in other words, how we feel? As a woman, you know that at any given time during a month, your emotions can be all over the place. Something that bothered you yesterday is acceptable today. Yesterday you were a bundle of tears, today you are a bundle of joy.

Many times, our emotional state will determine how we treat our husbands. It has little to do with what he "did" and a lot to do with how we are feeling. It does not seem like a good idea to let your emotions direct your behavior. This is why it is so important to have set limits on how we are going to act and react rather than letting the emotion of the day decide. Setting these limits are similar to making a vow to yourself, God, and others around you.

Psalm 76:11 Vow, and pay unto the LORD your God...

This vow or promise is what will direct your actions and reactions to any situation. You promise to yourself and to God that you will act in a certain way no matter how you are feeling. Decide now to set a personal standard of behavior that is non-negotiable. You could decide that you will not yell, you will not stomp out of the room, you will not accuse the other person, you will apologize for the things you did wrong, you will not crumble into tears, etc. This standard is based on godly principles of behavior and can be a foundation you can stand on when you feel emotional. It will keep your actions and reactions in check.

If you don't set a personal standard of behavior, the situation or fear will rule.

In Deuteronomy 7 Moses is asking the Children of Israel to set personal standards of behavior **_before_** they go into the promised land. In essence, he is saying, "Decide now who you are going to serve. Decide now how you are going to act." If they will not decide before they cross into the land, then the environment, the people, the situation, and emotion could potentially direct their actions and distract their hearts away from their God. Their affection will be pulled toward whatever is before their eyes.

Fear is what kept the Children of Israel out of the promised land the first time. Fear dictated their actions and kept them from moving forward into the land. Moses does not want that to happen to them again. He is asking for them to decide now how they will face situations and to decide to serve the Lord no matter what.

In Acts 7, Stephen did not let the situation rule. He had already set a personal standard of behavior before he ever stepped up to speak. If he had let the fear rule, he might not have said,

> **Acts 7:51** Ye stiffnecked and uncircumcised in heart and ears, ye do always resist the Holy Ghost: as your fathers *did*, so *do* ye.

Knowing that these words would incite violence against him, he might not have ever said these words. But Stephen knew these words needed to be said and he had decided to do what the Lord wanted without hesitation. Decide now to set a personal standard of behavior that is firm; unchanged by emotion, situation or fear.

Don't be enslaved and manipulated by any situation, emotions, and fear or let these factors dictate how you act. You do not want to be controlled by these things. You do not want to be manipulated. You can't let your heart decide your values because it has the potential to deceive you. Emotions are not always based in truth and thus you cannot trust them completely to guide your decisions and behavior. You can't let the moment decide how you are going to react because that moment will soon be over.

You can decide how you are going to act before you are in any situation. Decide now to establish a personal standard of behavior based on godly principles that will guide and dictate your actions and reactions.

Conversations

Have a Conversation with Your Lord Jesus

🙏 Lord, when was there a time that I let my emotions rule my behavior?

_____
_____

🙏 Lord, when was there a time where I let the situation change my behavior?

_____
_____

🙏 Lord, when was there a time when I decided how I was going to behave and resisted the temptation to behave otherwise?

_____
_____

🙏 Lord, I want to set a standard of behavior and decide now how I am going to act and react in any situation. I do not want to let my emotions and fear rule my behavior.

Pray...
_____
_____*...listen*

Face to Face With Your Lord

CONVERSATION 88

Night Torments

Related Bible Passages				
Old Testament	Psalms	Proverbs	New Testament
Deuteronomy 10	77	29	Acts 8

The night can be long and dark especially if your mind is filled with whirling thoughts of worry as you play out every detail of a situation in your mind. Fear and worry well up in tangible emotions as you consider every possible situation and how you would respond. As you lay in your bed you are not resting peacefully as you physically experience every possible situation as if it were real. You wonder where is God; has He forgotten to be gracious to you (Psalm 77:9)? You wake exhausted, feeling a dark cloud descending upon you.

> **Psalm 77:2-3** In the day of my trouble I sought the Lord: my sore ran in the night, and ceased not: my soul refused to be comforted. I remembered God, and was troubled: I complained, and my spirit was overwhelmed. Selah.

It is during these night torments that life situations start to get bigger and more powerful than your God. The situation has been allowed to grow to the point at which it seems beyond God's ability to intercede. You might ask, "Is his mercy clean gone for ever?" (Psalm 77:8) The situation is blinding you from God's presence and the fear of the situation or the fear of man is preventing you from holding on to your Lord's strength, power, and presence.

> **Proverbs 29:25** The fear of man bringeth a snare: but whoso putteth his trust in the LORD shall be safe.

Your fear of man or situation has you snared; snared from drawing close to the Lord for His guidance. This is when you put a man (or situation) in a position of influence where he does not belong. The "man" or "situation" is having more power in your life than your Lord. How do you release yourself from this snare and free yourself from these night torments of whirling thoughts?

Consider the worry and fear experienced by the early Christians in Saul's time (Acts 8). Before his conversion, Saul was persecuting the early Christians in horrible ways. He was a real and present threat to every Christian. Can you imagine going to bed each night tormented by the worry that you would be next?

> **Acts 8:3** As for Saul, he made havock of the church, entering into every house, and haling men and women committed *them* to prison.

Letting God be bigger than your fear of man in this situation would have been hard. In the face of this threat, putting your trust in your Lord Jesus would have been very difficult. But God was there. He was with these early Christians and He had a plan that furthered the gospel of Jesus Christ.

Acts 8:4 Therefore they that were scattered abroad went every where preaching the word.

In order to protect themselves, the people fled across the land and in doing so, they took the gospel of Jesus Christ with them. Many surrounding areas were exposed to the gospel of salvation that would not have been if those Christians had not fled to avoid persecution. God had a plan of deliverance and purpose in the crisis, but the people had to trust Him, look to Him for direction, and be able to receive His direction. Had they been snared by fear of situation or fear of man, they might have been too consumed with fear to see God's plan.

So, how do we release ourselves from this snare and free ourselves from these night torments of whirling thoughts? In YOUR time of torment, God has a plan for deliverance and purpose, but you have to put your trust in Him. You can't let "man" or "situation" get bigger than your God.

Search your heart and discover where "man" or "situation" has become a snare that is keeping you trapped and preventing you from trusting in your God. While in the night torment, the Psalmist started to calm the storm and release the snare when he decided to remember God's goodness.

Psalm 77:11-14 I will remember the works of the LORD: surely I will remember thy wonders of old. I will meditate also of all thy work, and talk of thy doings. Thy way, O God, *is* in the sanctuary: who *is so* great a God as *our* God? Thou *art* the God that doest wonders: thou hast declared thy strength among the people.

As you start to lift your eyes beyond "man" and "situation" and beyond your fear, worry, and anger you will start to see that God is your strength. God is your judge. God is your love. God has been there in the past and He is still with you now.

Deuteronomy 10:21 He *is* thy praise, and he *is* thy God, that hath done for thee these great and terrible things, which thine eyes have seen.

Conversations

Have a Conversation with Your Lord Jesus

༄ Lord, am I tormented by the "fear of man"?

_____
_____

༄ Lord, am I tormented by the "fear of situation"?

_____
_____

༄ Lord, am I letting a situation build fear in my thoughts? Am I tormenting myself with "what if"?

_____
_____

༄ Lord, I do not want to let "man" or "situation" become bigger than you. I do not want to be snared so that I cannot see you or follow you. Lord, help me to remember your greatness so that you are always bigger than my situation.

*Pray...*_____

_____*...listen*

Face to Face With Your Lord

CONVERSATION 89

Doubt and Deception

Related Bible Passages			
Old Testament	Psalms	Proverbs	New Testament
Deuteronomy 11	78	30	Acts 9

Deception is a horrible disease. The worst thing about the disease of deception is that you do not know you are diseased. It masks itself as truth; you will be convinced that everything is ok while deception corrupts your actions, reactions, and perception of God.

As I was considering deception and reading the passages from my Bible, I had to wonder if I was deceived in any way. Since it is cloaked to appear as truth, how was I going to discover if I was deceived? As I continued to talk to the Lord, some aspects of deception and how to identify it in my life became clearer.

How does deception get started? Doubting a truth about God is one major way deception enters and takes root. Doubt holds the door of our spirit wide open for deception to enter and harmonize with that doubt. Doubt opens the door for deception and then deception creates more doubt. This is a never-ending cycle that will move us farther and farther from our Lord as it continues to deteriorate the truth and power of the Lord in our life.

This cycle would be much easier to stop if we could identify deception in our own heart. Since it masquerades as truth, it is nearly impossible to identify it ourselves. Only the Word of God and the hand of God are capable of removing the hold of deception in our lives.

If you have deception in your heart, it can be revealed, and sometimes instantly. Consider Acts 9 and how Saul's deceived beliefs were confronted, revealed, and replaced with truth in a flash of light. In a moment of time, the Lord revealed himself, and Paul's beliefs were instantly changed. The deception in his heart was revealed and he was convinced and transformed.

> **Acts 9:17-18** And Ananias went his way, and entered into the house; and putting his hands on him said, Brother Saul, the Lord, *even* Jesus, that appeared unto thee in the way as thou camest, hath sent me, that thou mightest receive thy sight, and be filled with the Holy Ghost. And immediately there fell from his eyes as it had been scales: and he received sight forthwith, and arose, and was baptized.

Our Lord knows how we have been deceived. He can reveal it and expose what is hidden. I recently witnessed the Lord help a wonderful lady come to understand her deception. In a matter of days, she showed great strength by allowing the Word of God to rip at the shroud and reveal her deception. He then shined in truth to the point that she could not ignore it. It was beautiful to watch her countenance change in a moment as the deception was exposed and amputated, and truth took its place in her heart. It was transforming.

How do we keep the door of doubt shut so deception cannot enter? Faith, remembrance, and obedience are the keys to keeping the door of doubt shut.

> **Psalm 78:7-8** That they might set their hope in God, *[faith]* and not forget the works of God, *[remembrance]* but keep his commandments: *[obedience]* And might not be as their fathers, a stubborn and rebellious generation; a generation *that* set not their heart aright, and whose spirit was not stedfast with God.

Without faith, remembrance, and obedience doubt enters and deception follows. When deception takes root, stubbornness, rebellion, and a wavering spirit are the result.

Keeping doubt and deception from our spirit takes daily effort. We should not let a day go by that we don't spend time in God's word reminding ourselves of His greatness. We need to rest our faith in Him and align our heart with His commandments. We don't want to be deceived! It is a horrible disease of the spirit that we have little to no power to cure, but we have the power to prevent.

God's word has the power to keep doubt and deception out but also has the power to reveal the deception that already has taken root. In Deuteronomy, the Lord needed His people to have faith and obedience so that He could drive out all nations before them. These nations needed to be driven out of the land. They believed in other gods and would have become a snare of deception for His people. In the same way, the Lord needs us to have faith and obedience so He can reveal sources of deception and give us the strength to drive that doubt and deception far from us.

Deuteronomy 11:18-19 Therefore shall ye lay up these my words in your heart and in your soul, and bind them for a sign upon your hand, that they may be as frontlets between your eyes. And ye shall teach them your children, speaking of them when thou sittest in thine house, and when thou walkest by the way, when thou liest down, and when thou risest up.

Deuteronomy 11:22-23 For if ye shall diligently keep all these commandments which I command you, to do them, to love the LORD your God, to walk in all his ways, and to cleave unto him; Then will the LORD drive out all these nations from before you, and ye shall possess greater nations and mightier than yourselves.

Conversations

Have a Conversation with Your Lord Jesus

🌿 Lord, how might I be deceived?

_____
_____

🌿 Lord, what am I exposing myself to that might cause doubt and bring deception into my life?

_____
_____

🌿 Lord, what doubts do I have that might make it easy for deception to enter my understanding of you?

_____
_____

🌿 Lord, *"Remove far from me vanity and lies..." (Proverbs 30:8)* Reveal the deception in my heart and remove it. I want to rid my heart of all deception and doubt and I will replace it with faith in you, remembrance of your greatness, and obedience to your ways.

*Pray...*_____
_____
_____*...listen*

Face to Face With Your Lord

CONVERSATION 90

Me First

Related Bible Passages			
Old Testament	Psalms	Proverbs	New Testament
Deuteronomy 13	78	31	Acts 10

You would never follow a prophet that tells you of another God. You know enough about your God, that you would be able to tell when someone is trying to pull you away to worship a false god. You would never bow to an idol because you know that these objects have no power, are not God, and do not deserve your time and attention. It seems that it would be *very* easy to ignore a "prophet" that suggested you follow another God. But is the suggestion to follow another God subtler and more cloaked?

> **Deuteronomy 13:1-2** If there arise among you a prophet, or a dreamer of dreams, and giveth thee a sign or a wonder, And the sign or the wonder come to pass, whereof he spake unto thee, saying, Let us

go after other gods, which thou hast not known, and let us serve them;

As I considered this verse, I had to scoff a little at the audacity of being drawn to following after another god. I felt that I would have the sensibility to not fall for that lie. I would never see an idol as having any power and it does not represent the God in heaven. But then the Lord showed me that there is another god that is easy to follow after. This god is attractive and comforting. To drive home this concept, I asked myself if I had ever had any of the following thoughts:

- I don't have time to read my Bible.
- I am too tired to go to church today.
- It is too uncomfortable to go hand out tracts.
- I don't want to clean the church

The Lord showed me that those thoughts resonate from the voice of a false prophet saying, "Let us go serve the god of self-gratification, instead of the God of Heaven." Sadly, I had to admit that there had been times when I *had* followed the voice of a false profit.

Self-gratification is the act of pleasing or satisfying yourself, especially the gratifying of your own impulses, needs, or desires to the detriment of serving others including God. In many ways, self-gratification stands in opposition to the true definition of love. Love is so much more than an emotion or a feeling. Love is the action of putting aside your own wants and needs in order to meet the wants and desires of another.

So why does the false prophet that speaks up in our thoughts want us to feed self-gratification? Self-gratification is driven by a belief that we can do the job of meeting our own needs better than the Lord. It reasons that we must follow and fulfill our desires and needs first because no-one else will. Serving self-gratification eventually creates an insatiable monster that continually must have all needs and impulses met and this monster is never satisfied. In this state, there is no ability to show love because the individual is consumed with meeting their own needs.

When we give in to self-gratification rather than serving the Lord, we are in essence serving another god. In other words, you have made "you" more important in your life than God.

Psalm 78:30 blames the Israelites for not being "estranged from their lusts." Their drive for self-gratification and to fulfill their lusts set them at odds with the Lord. The Psalm goes on to say, "Therefore their days did he consume in vanity, and their years in trouble." (Psalm 78:33)

We do not have to be comfortable to serve the Lord; we do not have to be pain-free, we do not have to have everything in perfect order before we have time for the Lord or for showing others love. It is a decision to serve the Lord and others rather than serving self. In conjunction, it involves trusting Him to meet our needs.

What should we do when we hear that prophet in our head saying, "You don't need to do that today; you don't feel like it?"

> **Deuteronomy 13:3** Thou shalt not hearken unto the words of that prophet, or that dreamer of dreams: for the LORD your God proveth you, to know whether ye love the LORD your God with all your heart and with all your soul.

Our actions are evidence of our heart and our love for our Lord. A decision to put God's direction for our lives before our own agenda demonstrates our love for Him and this decision is recognized by God.

Acts 10:1-4 There was a certain man in Caesarea called Cornelius, a centurion of the band called the Italian *band, A* devout *man,* and one that feared God with all his house, which gave much alms to the people, and prayed to God alway. He saw in a vision evidently about the ninth hour of the day an angel of God coming in to him, and saying unto him, Cornelius. And when he looked on him, he was afraid, and said, What is it, Lord? And he said unto him, Thy prayers and thine alms are come up for a memorial before God.

God recognized Cornelius' devotion and it was memorialized before the Lord. He had the heart to serve God by overcoming the temptation to just serve self-gratification. God knows your motivation and He knows who you are serving.

Set aside your lusts, impulses, needs, and desires and put your attention and efforts on Him.

Proverbs 31:30 Favour *is* deceitful, and beauty *is* vain: *but* a woman *that* feareth the LORD, she shall be praised.

Be that woman that fears and serves the Lord rather than a woman that feeds and serves self-gratification. Be the woman that has the capacity to serve the Lord because she believes that He is able to meet her needs. Make the Lord the center of your purpose. Be estranged from your lusts and turn from the prophet that wants you to serve the god of self-gratification.

Conversations

Have a Conversation with Your Lord Jesus

  🕊 Lord, in what situations do I choose to serve myself rather than serving you?

_____

_____

  🕊 Lord, do I love you more than I love me?

_____

_____

  🕊 Lord, in what ways do I choose to serve you first with all my heart and with all my soul?

_____

_____

  🕊 Lord, when you take a peek into my life to prove me, what will you find? What god will you find me serving? Will I be serving the Lord Jesus or the god of self-gratification.

*Pray...*_____

_____*...listen*

Face to Face With Your Lord

CONVERSATION 91

Why is He Here?

Related Bible Passages			
Old Testament	Psalms	Proverbs	New Testament
Deuteronomy 15	78	1	Acts 11

You are at a party enjoying the fellowship of those you know and love. As you scan the crowd you notice someone who is out of place and was not invited! "Why is he here?" you ask as you cast an irritated glance his way. He is out of place and unwelcome. You wouldn't dare ask him to leave; he isn't causing any problems; he just is not welcome, so you just try to ignore his presence.

You notice the waiters going about serving and pleasing the guests. Their job is to meet your needs and they are doing it well. As you notice your empty cup you signal for their attention and one of the servers rush over to meet your need. Everyone is laughing, no one has a need, and everyone is content.

You notice the host. He is focused on each attendee as he gives his undivided attention to each person. You are proud to have been invited to his event. As he comes to speak to you, all of your attention and respect is given to him. He deserves it. As he speaks to you, you can tell he cares and invites your relationship. He is truly interested in you and you can sense his care. You are a guest in his house, yet you would have been pleased to have been invited to be a servant.

Now consider this, if this "party" is your life, is the Lord Jesus the unwelcome guest, a servant, or the host?

The Unwelcome Guest

Is the Lord an unwelcome guest in your life? Does he not fit in with the activities and friends that you hold dear? The Lord knows how you consider Him, and he knows what place he holds in your heart. Could he be saying the following about you?

> **Proverbs 1:24** Because I have called, and ye refused; I have stretched out my hand, and no man regarded;

If the Lord is a stranger to you, invite Him back into your life. Get to know Him better by spending time with Him. Regard His call and seek His face. Get to know Him so that you do not have to feel uncomfortable in His presence.

The Servant

Is the Lord present in your life only to meet your needs? Do you keep Him around to make your life better or to access when you have a need?

If that is the case the Lord knows your heart condition.

> **Psalm 78:36-37** Nevertheless they did flatter him with their mouth, and they lied unto him with their

tongues. For their heart was not right with him, neither were they stedfast in his covenant.

The Lord knows when He is just a tool in your life; just a servant at your party. He knows when you are keeping Him around just to serve your purposes.

Can you envision your Lord standing before you with His hand outstretched and the following conversation taking place? "Dear child, let's talk!" And you respond with, "Not now Lord. I have no need."

Ideally, your heart needs to be receptive to the Lord's voice even while in a state of fullness and contentment. The Lord is not a servant in your life. He is so much more!

The Host

> **Deuteronomy 15:5-6** Only if thou carefully hearken unto the voice of the LORD thy God, to observe to do all these commandments which I command thee this day. For the LORD thy God blesseth thee, as he promised thee: and thou shalt lend unto many nations, but thou shalt not borrow; and thou shalt reign over many nations, but they shall not reign over thee.

As the host of your life, the Lord is given honor, appreciation, respect, and responsiveness. He is in control and you would gladly do His bidding to show your reverence. Your life is His event and you are in attendance rather than seeing yourself as the organizer of the event and the Lord is an intruder or at best a servant.

In Acts 11 you see that the Lord is the host of Peter's life. The Lord has a special job for Peter to do and he responded with a willingness to be used by the Lord.

Acts 11:17 Forasmuch then as God gave them the like gift as *he did* unto us, who believed on the Lord Jesus Christ; what was I, that I could withstand God?

Peter was directed by God to go and deliver the gospel of Jesus Christ to an Italian centurion and his family. Peter did not hesitate, and many were saved because of his willingness to go. In fact, Peter remarks, "...what was I, that I could withstand God?" Peter was willing to serve his host.

Consider your relationship with the Lord. God is so much more than a servant and He certainly should not be considered an intruder in your life. He is God, the creator of this world, your Savior, and He desires to be your friend and guide. He loves you and wants a relationship with you.

Constant, consistent, close, caring; these words describe His heart toward you. May these same words be used to describe your heart to your Lord.

Conversations

Have a Conversation with Your Lord Jesus

- Lord, are you an unwelcome guest, a servant, or the host in my life?

  _____
  _____

- Lord, what kind of relationship do you want with me?

  _____
  _____

- Lord, how do I keep you out of parts of my life?

  _____
  _____

- Lord, you are welcome in my life and I desire for you to be the organizer and leader of my life. I am honored to attend and be your servant rather than expecting you to be mine.

  *Pray...*_____
  _____
  _____*...listen*

Face to Face With Your Lord

CONVERSATION 92

Which Way?

Related Bible Passages			
Old Testament	Psalms	Proverbs	New Testament
Deuteronomy 17	78	2	Acts 13

As you walk along the path of life you will see many possible paths to follow and many decisions to make. You will choose different ways because they look good or feel right. When you are faced with a decision, you might ask yourself, "Which way do I go; what should I do?"

Sometimes I have felt that it can be impossible to know if I am making the right decision especially if I have no specific direction from God. However, through this conversation, God showed me that with Him as my guide, I can have confidence that He is guiding me through these decisions. Primarily, I will receive this guidance through being involved in God's word and through having a relationship with my Savior. My devotion to staying close to Him will pull me onto the right path. As I am reading, seeking and finding a message for each day, He is pulling and guiding my heart in the right direction.

The king in Deuteronomy 17 knew how important it was for him to be close to God's word and to maintain a close relationship with his guide. So, as he read, he wrote a copy so that God's word would be with him. He made God's word flow through him as he read to understand.

> **Deuteronomy 17:18-20** And it shall be, when he sitteth upon the throne of his kingdom, that he shall write him a copy of this law in a book out of *that which is* before the priests the Levites: And it shall be with him, and he shall read therein all the days of his life: that he may learn to fear the LORD his God, to keep all the words of this law and these statutes, to do them: That his heart be not lifted up above his brethren, and that he turn not aside from the commandment, *to* the right hand, or *to* the left: to the end that he may prolong *his* days in his kingdom, he, and his children, in the midst of Israel.

The result of his devotion was that he learned to fear. This is not a fear related to trepidation; it is a fear that is related to respect for the Lord his God. Without fear of the Lord, we will continue to choose whatever path looks and feels good to us and then expect the Lord to follow along. In this situation, the path we choose will feel right for a moment, but we will soon realize that our impulsive action has undesirable consequences.

> **Psalm 78:56-58** Yet they tempted and provoked the most high God, and kept not his testimonies: But turned back, and dealt unfaithfully like their fathers: they were turned aside like a deceitful bow. For they provoked him to anger with their high places, and moved him to jealousy with their graven images.

Conversations

The wanderers in the verse above "turned back" and "turned aside" from following God. They were wandering through life, without direction and choosing the wrong path because they did not take God as their guide. In doing so they tempted and provoked God. Can you imagine tempting and provoking the most high God? This seems beyond imaginable. However, if you allow yourself to wander away from His direction, you could be making decisions that go directly against the Lord. You will provoke Him!

In addition, by being close to God's word, the king learned to not lift his heart above his brethren. It is so easy to look down on those that have different thoughts and ways. When we look down on others, it artificially elevates us. God tells us to not esteem ourselves better than another and staying close to His word keeps us in a position to love the people around us. When we esteem ourselves better than another, we have already stepped off the path that the Lord wants us on. We have wandered to a place where the Lord did not lead.

The king also knew that his heart was prone to wander and stray off course and away from the Lord. This will happen to us too if we don't put in place mechanisms to bind our heart to the Lord's. Your life is a dark room, your Bible is the light, and the Lord is your guide. Cling to your relationship with Him and you will find your way.

In Acts, we see Paul and Barnabas serving the Lord and preaching God's word. These two men delivered a powerful message to the Jews.

> **Acts 13:42** And when the Jews were gone out of the synagogue, the Gentiles besought that these words might be preached to them the next sabbath.

The gentiles could not wait to hear the same message that the Jew's had heard. They knew it was a wonderful message of hope and guidance. They hungered after the Lord. Do you have a desire for time with your Lord and hunger to know more?

It is so important for us to be in God's word every day! It keeps Him moving through our lives and thoughts. Without Him, we will start to make decisions that do not consider God's ways. Being in God's word every day we are reminded to fear the Lord our God. We are given a correct self-image, and we are returned to a path that brings glory to God.

Don't waste your Bible reading time by passively reading the words that present themselves before you. Read with attention and expectancy. These words truly are living words and will have a profound effect on your life if you will get involved and pay attention when you read your Bible. God has a message for you.

> **Proverbs 2:3-5** Yea, if thou criest after knowledge, *and* liftest up thy voice for understanding; If thou seekest her as silver, and searchest for her as *for* hid treasures; Then shalt thou understand the fear of the LORD, and find the knowledge of God.

Conversations

Have a Conversation with Your Lord Jesus

🕯 Lord, are you my guide or am I walking alone?

_____
_____

🕯 Lord, what do I do to keep myself close to you?

_____
_____

🕯 Lord, when I have a decision to make, how often do I seek your guidance?

_____
_____

🕯 Lord, I want to bind my heart to yours. I desire to stay close to you, so I can know you are guiding me through life's decisions.

   Pray...
   _____
   _____
   _____*...listen*

Face to Face With Your Lord

CONVERSATION 93

It is Not God's Fault

Related Bible Passages			
Old Testament	Psalms	Proverbs	New Testament
Deuteronomy 20	79	3	Acts 14

God has supreme and ultimate power over everything. True? So, if God loves you and has knowledge and control over all things, why doesn't He stop bad things from happening?

Unfortunately, Christians are not exempt from experiencing the natural processes of this world; Christians get to experience the physiological and natural systems in this sin-cursed world just like everyone else.

If this fact is ignored, it might appear that God seems to protect one person, but not another. You will hear of people talking about how God delivered, blessed or protected them yet you stand there tormented by life. This might lead you to ask, "Why isn't God helping me? Why did God let this happen to me? He could have stopped it! Why didn't He protect me!!?"

Psalm 79:5 How long, LORD? wilt thou be angry for ever? shall thy jealousy burn like fire?

If you are in this state, you might feel compelled to ask God "Why?" but this is not an innocent question. This question comes with strings attached to serious assumptions. This question is formed out of a subconscious belief that your pain and difficulty is God's fault; in asking this question you believe He is the originator of your pain by causing it in some way, or He could have prevented it if He wanted to. Why is this assumption harmful? Because it is human nature to avoid pain, and if you believe that God is the instigator of pain in your life, you might inadvertently avoid Him.

The Lord brought this conversation to me at the perfect time after our church building experienced a major fire. It happened late at night so the fire had time to spread and do major damage before someone noticed. It was significant. When I saw the damage, I was shocked. It hit me hard. We had put so much time, effort and love into physically building that building. I couldn't imagine having to do it again. I heard people say, "I wonder why God did this," or, "God must have a plan for allowing this." Neither of these statements settled well with me. I did not want to make this tragedy God's fault. All I knew was that God was going to help us through this.

So why do bad things happen? It is because of nature, sin, and consequence.

We live in a physical, tangible world and we are at the mercy of nature and biology. We can't jump off a building and expect that God would save us. Gravity wins. We will catch colds during the cold-and-flu season. It is not an indicator of the lack of God's protection in our lives, it is biology. When nature and biology cause difficulty in our lives, it is wrong to assume that God should push aside this natural world for our convenience. Why do bad things happen? Because of nature. It's not God's fault.

We might be touched by the sin of others. Our lives can be made miserable because someone near to us refuses to listen to God and change. Is our misery God's fault? No. God is not going to force anyone beyond their will. In Acts 14:19 Paul is stoned because the people refused to believe. Did Paul blame God for the near-death beating that he sustained? No. Was it God's *will* that he be stoned? No. Paul understood the source of his trial. God was not going to force these people to believe and Paul experienced the result of their unbelief and anger. People have the volition to do bad things, and unfortunately, we might feel the effects of their choices. God, however, *can* and *will* use the situation for His glory. Why do bad things happen? Because of sin. It's not God's fault.

We might be experiencing trials because of our sin. Every decision we make comes with consequences; pleasant and unpleasant. With unhealthy decisions come uncomfortable consequences. God is not going to force us to do right; God is not going to force us to listen or change, but He will reward us for our actions regardless.

> **Proverbs 3:11-12** My son, despise not the chastening of the LORD; neither be weary of his correction: For whom the LORD loveth he correcteth; even as a father the son *in whom* he delighteth.

Because of our decisions, we might be experiencing unpleasant consequences and that is the Lord lovingly changing our course and bringing us to change our mind about our decisions. If we are going through difficulty because of the guiding hand of God, then it is because of our wayward decisions. A loving parent will correct her child because his actions are harmful to him and others, so why would we believe that God would be any different? It is not the parent's fault that the child is corrected and guided. It is the child's actions that needed correction and guidance.

A peaceful, happy life is everyone's objective, but it is not an indicator of God's love for us. Our contentment or happiness is not a scale that measures God's love for us. In the same way, hard times and pain are not an indicator of the absence of God.

> **Deuteronomy 20:4** For the LORD your God *is* he that goeth with you, to fight for you against your enemies, to save you.

God is with you and you have the privilege to have Him by your side as you experience the pains and joys of this world. This is how you know God loves you because He promised to be with you.

Don't deceive yourself by believing your trial is His fault. This will cause you to distance yourself from your only true source of comfort, help, and guidance. Don't go through life alone because you believe that God has forsaken you. Don't miss God's deliverance because you are blaming Him for the trial.

So, what should you do when faced with disaster and disease? Draw near to God.

What should you do when you experience someone's anger? Draw near to God.

What should you do if you feel the guiding hand of God because of your unhealthy decisions? Draw near to God.

Conversations

Have a Conversation with Your Lord Jesus

☙ Lord, have I blamed you for my discomfort?

_____
_____

☙ Lord, when I have felt pain and difficulty, who or what was at fault?

_____
_____

☙ Lord, how will blaming you taint my relationship with you?

_____
_____

☙ Lord, I know you are true and just; you are also caring and loving. In my trial and discomfort, I want to draw closer to you and not believe anything that will cause me to run from you.

*Pray...*_____
_____
...listen

Face to Face With Your Lord

CONVERSATION 94

Pure Religion

Related Bible Passages				
Old Testament	Psalms	Proverbs	New Testament
Deuteronomy 22	80	4	James 1

What is pure religion? This is a hard question because the definition has the potential to vary greatly with everyone.

The best definition of pure religion is not found in personal interpretation. Some might say that pure religion is going to church every Sunday, and some might say it is belonging to the right church or following the ideals of the right person. Personal interpretations have the potential to corrupt the essence of pure religion. The best definition of pure religion is found in your Bible. God has defined pure religion for you.

> **James 1:27** Pure religion and undefiled before God and the Father is this, To visit the fatherless and widows in their affliction, *and* to keep himself unspotted from the world.

Pure religion is not a mere philosophy bound by ritual and rules, it is defined by a relationship with Jesus Christ, service towards others, and in how you are honoring God through your life. In this conversation, the Lord had me consider how I am exercising religion based on His definition. I fear that at times, I have added to His definition and created a "religion" that was not God's design. I want to worship God that way that He has designed.

To visit the fatherless

Pure religion is demonstrated by serving others in need. Have you ever avoided helping someone because it was inconvenient or difficult? Have you ever helped one person but not another because they did not "deserve" your help? I can remember a few times where I have been guilty of this. Everyone is guilty at one point in time of withholding help because of any number of excuses.

> **James 2:8-9** If ye fulfil the royal law according to the scripture, Thou shalt love thy neighbour as thyself, ye do well: But if ye have respect to persons, ye commit sin, and are convinced of the law as transgressors.

To have "respect to persons" means to help one but not another because you perceive that one deserves your help and the other does not. This justification is not God-honoring. The evidence of our love for the Lord is found in our helpful actions to everyone. It is helping everyone the Lord puts in our path to help without assessing worthiness before giving aid. The person doesn't have to be a close friend; they do not have to deserve it or return the favor. We help because we love our Lord.

Have you ever turned away when someone needs help, or walked the other way, avoided eye contact, or ignored her request for help? Maybe instead of lending physical help, you simply said, "I will pray for you," when it was within your capacity to offer physical help as well as prayer. Notice in the verse below that the friend "hid" so that he did not have to help.

> **Deuteronomy 22:1-2** Thou shalt not see thy brother's ox or his sheep go astray, and hide thyself from them: thou shalt in any case bring them again unto thy brother. And if thy brother *be* not nigh unto thee, or if thou know him not, then thou shalt bring it unto thine own house, and it shall be with thee until thy brother seek after it, and thou shalt restore it to him again.

Helping someone is rarely convenient. It is easy to come up with a reason not to help. Because of our love for God, we can be ready to inconvenience ourselves to help someone. We should not be choosy, hide or ignore anyone's plea. Help, serve, and love others. This is pure religion.

To keep himself unspotted from the world

Pure religion is also defined by how we live; our morals and standards. It is so easy to get sucked into the "normal." We are surrounded by the world and it is easy for the worldly views and philosophies to become "normal" and acceptable. When these views are compared to the Bible, it becomes clear that they are not compatible with a godly perspective.

> **Psalm 80:19** Turn us again, O LORD God of hosts, cause thy face to shine; and we shall be saved.

Living with worldly principles turns us away from the Lord. It turns our mind, body, and spirit away for our Lord. In this state, we have headed in another direction away from our loving Lord. We need to turn around; turn our life around so our principles and morals are aligned with God's. This is pure religion.

> **Proverbs 4:25-27** Let thine eyes look right on, and let thine eyelids look straight before thee. Ponder the path of thy feet, and let all thy ways be established. Turn not to the right hand nor to the left: remove thy foot from evil.

Today, the Lord reminded me to exercise pure religion. He revealed ways that I am not exercising my love for Him. I want to renew my love for my Lord. I desire to receive those I can help and live my life in a way that shows my appreciation for what the Lord Jesus Christ has done for me. This is pure religion. How about you? Are you ready to live pure religion?

Conversations

Have a Conversation with Your Lord Jesus

🕯 Lord, do I exercise pure religion as defined by you?

_____
_____

🕯 Lord, have I ever avoided helping someone you gave me to help?

_____
_____

🕯 Lord, what changes do I need to make to my life so that I keep myself "unspotted from the world?"

_____
_____

🕯 Lord, I want to practice pure religion. I want to receive those that need help and not hide from them. I want to honor you in the way I act.

Pray...
_____
_____
...listen

Face to Face With Your Lord

CONVERSATION 95

Be Kind

Related Bible Passages			
Old Testament	Psalms	Proverbs	New Testament
Deuteronomy 24	81	5	James 3

"Be kind!" It sounds so easy, however, displaying kindness all the time is definitely easier said than done. It is easy to be nice when others around you are being nice, but what happens when they are crabby, they challenge you, or do not perform the way you want? Returning kindness in these situations can be very difficult. It is almost like some people consider kindness to be a reward they give when things are going their way. When things are not going their way, then they feel justified in being unkind. As you can imagine, your Lord has something to say about our display of kindness.

> **James 3:14-16** But if ye have bitter envying and strife in your hearts, glory not, and lie not against the truth. This wisdom descendeth not from above, but

is earthly, sensual, devilish. For where envying and strife *is*, there *is* confusion and every evil work.

Unkindness can erupt because of many different situations in a person's life, however, two strong factors are when this person is harboring bitter envying and strife. Justifying our unkindness is a lie we tell ourselves. We might justify our unkindness by believing the other person deserved it. We might justify our unkind behavior because the other person was unkind to us. No matter our justification, God calls our unkind behavior "earthly, sensual, devilish." There simply is no place for unkindness if you are a child of God and trying to honor Him.

It is true that some people are just naturally kind while others find it more of a challenge. It might be easier for them to maintain kindness in difficult situations. While this might be true, it does not relieve us from our responsibility to have more control over our display of kindness.

Why is being kind so important to God? As I had this conversation with the Lord, I asked why does my behavior matter? Why is it important to God how I act? It sounds like a silly question; of course, we should be nice. However, these verses made me wonder if there was a deeper reason. As I read through the related verses, it became clear. It is because He desires for me to draw others toward me, so I can be a conduit of His love in their lives. By others being drawn closer to me, they are being drawn closer to Christ because He is in me. How I act towards others will either draw them closer to me or push them away. I want to be kind; I want to be nice to others so I can show others Christ's love that he has given to me to pass on.

James 3:17-18 But the wisdom that is from above is first pure, then peaceable, gentle, *and* easy to be intreated, full of mercy and good fruits, without partiality, and without hypocrisy. And the fruit of righteousness is sown in peace of them that make peace.

Kindness is a tool we use to make peace. Kindness is a gentle, peaceable, and approachable disposition. Anything short of pure kindness and we are kindling strife. Bitter envying and strife walk hand-in-hand with a hateful attitude and our "beast" comes out to consume the person that has caused distress. This unkindness does not reflect Christ; it does not draw others toward Him and it does not create peace.

Unfortunately, we cannot just decide to be kind and suddenly it happens. Kindness is born from the heart condition. To truly be kind we have to identify and deal with bitter envying and strife in our heart.

In my conversation with the Lord, I felt Him asking me the following questions. Do you see weaknesses or transgressions in someone's life and feel the need to play the role of the Holy Spirit in her life by not being nice to her? Are you disgusted by the presence of someone? Has someone disappointed you? I had to admit that there had been times that had done this.

There is a tendency to conclude that being unkind and distant will convict a person of their wrong-doing. This seems ridiculous, but I know I have been guilty of this absurd plan. I need to let God convict others of their bad choices. My job is to be kind to others.

Proverbs 5:22 His own iniquities shall take the wicked himself, and he shall be holden with the cords of his sins.

Sometimes a person is not kind because she wants to keep people away. Someone hurt her or disappointed her once, and it is safer to keep people at a distance. This is accomplished by not being nice. If this might be your story, let God take your burden of hurt so you can be kind. Let the Lord be your defender. Stop punishing others for something someone else did. Let someone be nice to you and you return the gift.

> **Psalm 81:6-7** I removed his shoulder from the burden: his hands were delivered from the pots. Thou calledst in trouble, and I delivered thee; I answered thee in the secret place of thunder: I proved thee at the waters of Meribah. Selah.

It is a huge burden to carry around a past offense. Stop being "hurt" and feeling offended; give the burden to the Lord so you are free to be kind and draw others toward God.

Even in personal conflict, God has an expectation that we would be kind. Just because we are in a disagreement with a friend or our husbands, does not give us the liberty to act however we want. We still have to be kind. We still have to reflect God. How do you treat God's family when you are in conflict? Have you been nice, or did you take advantage of the situation and "speak your mind?" God wants us to be nice even during conflict.

Being kind is a gift you give with no expectations.

> **Deuteronomy 24:20** When thou beatest thine olive tree, thou shalt not go over the boughs again: it shall be for the stranger, for the fatherless, and for the widow.

God tells the gardener to not glean twice, to leave some olives for the poor and fatherless. There is no return for his kindness. The widows and fatherless will come, take of the olives, and leave. God expects him to be kind anyway. The kindness we display to others is shown in the same way. Our kindness is an undeserved gift we give to someone else with no promise of return. Sometimes we are so stingy. We will only display kindness if it is purchased, deserved, or reciprocated. If this is the situation, kindness is no longer a gift; it has become merchandise.

Be kind! It is easier than you think when you get rid of envying and strife and replace it with thankfulness and joy.

Face to Face With Your Lord

Have a Conversation with Your Lord Jesus

☙ Lord, in what situations do I find it hard to be kind?

_____
_____

☙ Lord, how do others hear my words and my tone? Do they hear peace and kindness?

_____
_____

☙ Lord, am I harboring bitter envying and strife in my heart?

_____
_____

☙ Lord, I want to be kind to others for your glory. Please help me to identify why I am not kind in certain situations and replace that heart condition with one that will produce kindness.

Pray... _____

_____
_____ *...listen*

CONVERSATION 96

Be Doing

Related Bible Passages			
Old Testament	Psalms	Proverbs	New Testament
Deuteronomy 27	82	6	Acts 15

As soon as the Israelites crossed over the Jordan River, they were to commemorate the accomplishment by setting up stones in the form of an altar as a physical reminder of all that God had done for them and a reminder of His commandments.

> **Deuteronomy 27:4** Therefore it shall be when ye be gone over Jordan, *that* ye shall set up these stones, which I command you this day...

> **Deuteronomy 27:7-8** And thou shalt offer peace offerings, and shalt eat there, and rejoice before the LORD thy God. And thou shalt write upon the stones all the words of this law very plainly.

What if you were to do the same thing; build an altar of stones that would represent all that the Lord has done for you? Upon looking at it, others could tell how great your God is. They would know His commandments and they would also be reminded of His love for them. This altar of stones would confirm many truths about the Lord to the observer. It would also be a place for conversations about the Lord to begin.

"What does this stone represent?"

"Oh! That one is when the Lord led me to help a woman through a difficult time."

"What about this one?"

"Well, that was when the Lord gave me direction and helped me make an important decision."

Now, I know that the Lord does not want us to start construction on a great stone monolith for Him. But what He does want us to do is live a life that is a memorial to Him. We can build a grand memorial to Him daily in the things we do. The greatest memorial and testament to His commandments is found in how we act, in how we live our lives, and in our willingness to reach out to others. The memorial to God is built on how we represent Him.

> **Psalms 82:3-4** Defend the poor and fatherless: do justice to the afflicted and needy. Deliver the poor and needy: rid *them* out of the hand of the wicked.

God needs us to be His hands and we memorialize Him through our willingness.

Building our memorial to the Lord starts with the heart and ends in our actions. Great actions cannot come out of a bitter disposition. In essence, our actions are the physical manifestation of our spiritual condition. If we want to build a great memorial to our Lord by what we do, then we have to first take heed to our spirit. Being healthy spiritually gives us the proper foundation to build a grand memorial for the Lord through our actions.

As I considered my "memorial" to the Lord, I knew it had to start with my obedience to Him. I want to follow His direction. Are there things that I know the Lord has told me to stop, and I haven't yet? Are there things that I know the Lord has told me to do, and I haven't started yet? Now is the time. I need to just do it.

Every Christian has a call to create disciples for the Lord. We are to introduce others to Him. What we are doing will either draw others to Him or turn them away. We can have an astounding knowledge of the Lord, but what we do will ultimately be the element that has an impact on someone's life. Do right. It matters. With everything we DO, we are adding to our memorial for our Lord.

In Acts, Paul wanted to go check up on those he had led to the Lord.

> **Acts 15:36** And some days after Paul said unto Barnabas, Let us go again and visit our brethren in every city where we have preached the word of the Lord, *and see* how they do.

He wanted to make an observation of actions. Certainly, they were going to make sure the brethren were "believing" the right doctrine, but ultimately, they wanted to make sure they were acting out the doctrine and living the faith.

We can start building something grand and beautiful for the Lord. Our memorial to Him will be amazing because every day we will place on another stone by doing something for Him and recognizing what He has done for us.

> **Proverbs 6:20-22** My son, keep thy father's commandment, and forsake not the law of thy mother:

Bind them continually upon thine heart, and tie them about thy neck. When thou goest, it shall lead thee; when thou sleepest, it shall keep thee; and when thou awakest, it shall talk with thee.

Conversations

Have a Conversation with Your Lord Jesus

ༀ Lord, what is stopping me from doing something for you each day?

_____
_____

ༀ Lord, what are some things that I can do for you?

_____
_____

ༀ Lord, is there something I need to stop doing?

_____
_____

ༀ Lord, I want my life to be a living memorial for you. I want people to see you through what I do.

*Pray...*_____
_____
_____*...listen*

Face to Face With Your Lord

CONVERSATION 97

Overtaken

Related Bible Passages			
Old Testament	Psalms	Proverbs	New Testament
Deuteronomy 28	83	7	Galatians 1

Walking along the shore at sunset with my husband was a perfect and serene experience. I felt the water softly lapping at my feet. It was a calm, beautiful evening and the sun was slowly settling on the horizon. With my attention on the setting sun, I failed to recognize that the waves were gaining strength. As I walked my attention was on the setting sun, and I had no way to anticipate what was about to happen.

Without warning, a powerful wave surfaced and rushed into me. I was knocked to the sand and engulfed by the water. The retreating wave grabbed at me attempting to pull me back into the ocean with it. There was nothing I could do. Once I had been overtaken by the wave all I could do was experience its power and try to fight for something to hang on to. Grabbing onto the thinning sand I was able to withstand the force and not be fully pulled under. Before the next wave hit, I was able to crawl to safety; away from the next attack. I sat on the sand amazed at the suddenness and power of that wave. It was completely unexpected, and I had no way to prepare. I had been overtaken.

There are events in our life that we cannot escape or prevent. Things happen that are so sudden, powerful and consequential that we can be overtaken by their immensity. The situation is relentless, prevailing and all-consuming. We become trapped in the turmoil. Powers have come upon us and we cannot get away; all we can do is scramble to survive or be drowned and consumed.

Have you ever been overtaken? Do you remember drowning in fear, pain, sorrow, depression, or hopelessness? You felt trapped in a horrible situation where there was no way out. In this condition, you can try to survive, but you can't escape; you feel like you are barely holding on, and you have no control. As a Christian, you know that your Lord is the only one that can reach into the torrent and pull you out. He is the only one that can rescue you and guide when you have been overtaken.

The Bible also speaks of being overtaken; overtaken by curses and blessings. We might experience an overwhelming time in our life that causes us to shift our attention back to our Lord; to seek His face and to seek His hand. It is also possible that the overwhelming situation will remind us that we need Him.

> **Deuteronomy 28:15** But it shall come to pass, if thou wilt not hearken unto the voice of the LORD thy God, to observe to do all his commandments and his statutes which I command thee this day; that all these curses shall come upon thee, and overtake thee:

Deuteronomy 28:47 Because thou servedst not the LORD thy God with joyfulness, and with gladness of heart, for the abundance of all *things*;

In calm and easy times, it is common for a person to lose touch with the Lord; unfortunate but it does happen. When need and trouble are not present, a person can stray from her relationship with the Lord. This is easily seen in the lives of the Israelites. They then experienced Lord trials and difficulty that caused them to shift their attention back to Him.

Psalm 83:15-16 So persecute them with thy tempest, and make them afraid with thy storm. Fill their faces with shame; that they may seek thy name, O LORD.

Why will God allow these tempests? Why does He want us to hearken to Him and draw near to Him? It is because, He knows there is no mercy in this world, no guidance, no wisdom, and no real contentment and joy. When we get distracted by this world and our attention away from serving Him, we are building trust and a relationship with this world rather than with Him. Our Lord Jesus knows that will ultimately destroy us and He wants to prevent that from happening.

Galatians 1:4 Who gave himself for our sins, that he might deliver us from this present evil world, according to the will of God and our Father:

He delights in a relationship with you. He wants to bless you. He loves you and wants to rescue you, guide you, and protect you.

Proverbs 7:24-25 Hearken unto me now therefore, O ye children, and attend to the words of my mouth. Let not thine heart decline to her ways, go not astray in her paths.

The Bible also speaks of being overtaken by another force. Rather than being overtaken by curses, the Bible speaks of being overtaken by blessings.

> **Deuteronomy 28:1-2** And it shall come to pass, if thou shalt hearken diligently unto the voice of the LORD thy God, to observe *and* to do all his commandments which I command thee this day, that the LORD thy God will set thee on high above all nations of the earth: And all these blessings shall come on thee, and overtake thee, if thou shalt hearken unto the voice of the LORD thy God.

The recipe for being overtaken by the Lord's blessing is if we will "hearken diligently" to His commandments, "observe" and "do" them! Even when we are being overtaken by life's troubles and terrors, we can still experience being overtaken by the Lord's blessings. Stay very close to Him, follow His commandments and do those things that bring a smile to His face.

What joy! Imagine being overtaken, not in terror, but in the Lord's blessing. Being totally consumed and surrounded, not by worry or fear, but by love, peace, and contentment. Wouldn't it be incredible; something so prevailing and wonderful that you find yourself completely consumed and overtaken by the power of the Lord's blessing.

Conversations

Have a Conversation with Your Lord Jesus

෪ Lord, when I have been overtaken by trouble, what did I reach out to for help?

_____
_____
_____

෪ Lord, when times are good, do I stay close to you?

_____
_____
_____

෪ Lord, how do I daily renew my relationship with you?

_____
_____
_____

෪ Lord, I want to stay close to you. I want to be near to the one that can rescue me when life gets hard. Thank you for overtaking me with your blessings.

Pray...
_____
_____
...listen

Face to Face With Your Lord

CONVERSATION 98

I Know!

| Related Bible Passages ||||
Old Testament	Psalms	Proverbs	New Testament
Deuteronomy 29	84	8	Galatians 4

Have you ever given someone instruction and she refused it? In fact, she deflected it with an indignant, "I know!" It was obvious to you she needed the advice or direction, but this new information was not welcome. She felt the need to defend herself by declaring, "I know!"

I have to confess, this is a pet-peeve of mine. I am in a conversation with someone and I have some information for them that I know is new to them. Their response, "I know!" is something that makes my skin crawl. As I contemplated this irritation, the Lord reminded me that I am also guilty of this. There have been times that I have been threatened by not having the right information, so in defense, I have declared, "I know!" In this conversation, the Lord has shown me how dangerous this attitude is and how the disease of knowing is a threat to my growth.

Have you ever felt threatened by new information and declared "I know?" It is important to recognize that by declaring "I know", we are not sending the message that we have knowledge, but rather we are communicating that we have suspended our learning and we have closed the door to new instruction or direction.

By declaring "I know", we are communicating that the instruction we just received was not necessary, not welcome, and we need no further information.

> **Proverbs 8:33** Hear instruction, and be wise, and refuse it not.

This command from God is clear. We are to always be in a mindset to receive new information. Declaring "I know" is the refusal to receive new information. "I know" means nothing else is coming in; we are closed. This defensive attitude ultimately creates the disease of knowing. This is where we come to believe that we know everything and that no new information is necessary. When we fall into this trap, curiosity is strangled and a part of us that needs to grow begins to die. We suffocate all learning.

> **Galatians 4:3-5** Even so we, when we were children, were in bondage under the elements of the world: But when the fulness of the time was come, God sent forth his Son, made of a woman, made under the law, To redeem them that were under the law, that we might receive the adoption of sons.

Consider when you were still "in bondage under the elements of the world." Someone came into your life and presented to you the gospel of Christ. You knew you needed that new information and received it. If you would have declared "I know" upon being presented with the gospel, you would have missed learning about the gift of salvation. You would have remained shrouded in your lack of understanding and missed a new knowledge of Christ.

Aren't you glad you did not declare, "I know!" when someone started to present the Gospel of Jesus Christ? But what other messages from God have you missed because you declared, "I know!" when you felt threatened by new information?

When we declare "I know" we lose our curiosity. Curiosity is an open and inquisitive mind that does not already believe that it knows. Think about when you were a new Christian. You had a beginner's mind that was enlightened and awakened. You were curious about God and anything about Him. As a new Christian, you would have never declared "I know," you would have said, "Tell me more!"

> **Psalm 84:2** My soul longeth, yea, even fainteth for the courts of the LORD: my heart and my flesh crieth out for the living God.

As a mature Christian, we have to keep growing and learning in order to fight the disease of knowing. We do not know all there is to know about our Lord or how the Lord desires for us to change. We still need to learn and grow. Don't stop.

> **Deuteronomy 29:29** The secret *things belong* unto the LORD our God: but those *things which are* revealed *belong* unto us and to our children for ever, that *we* may do all the words of this law.

The way to continue growing is certainly not through declaring, "I know" and it isn't necessarily through just "thinking" more. It's through having experiences, keeping our curiosity and asking questions. It is through listening to others and considering their direction and advice. It is through observing something new that teaches us something we didn't know.

Don't let yourself get to the point of believing that you already know everything you need to know or get to where your defenses want to deflect new instruction. Some things have to come by digging, learning, searching, and being told.

Declaring "I know" does not mean that you really have arrived at understanding, it really only reveals that you are done learning.

Conversations

Have a Conversation with Your Lord Jesus

🕊 Lord, have I missed instruction because I am convinced that I already know?

_____
_____

🕊 Lord, have I missed instruction because I am convinced that I already know?

_____
_____

🕊 Lord, show me something new and amazing.

_____
_____

🕊 Lord, I want to be open and curious about you and be ready to learn more.

*Pray...*_____

_____
                                          ...listen

Face to Face With Your Lord

CONVERSATION 99

I Have a Pattern

Related Bible Passages				
Old Testament	Psalms	Proverbs	New Testament
Deuteronomy 32	85	9	Galatians 5

I have noticed that once someone is in a pattern of behavior, it is very difficult for that person to change. Bad behavior, especially, seems to be more resistant to change than good behavior. I have noticed this in myself. I can identify a habit or trait that I want to change and it takes exhaustive effort to make the change.

Many times, criminals go to prison for their bad deeds and return to society just to commit them again. In a like manner, we will be convicted of sin, confess it to the Lord, determine to change and shortly find ourselves guilty again. It is a pattern for sin that is so difficult to break. Consider someone that frequently tells lies or someone who is given to anger. These people are struggling with a pattern of sin. They may know what they are doing is wrong, they desire to change, but after reflecting on their response to a situation, they realize they have fallen into their old pattern of sin.

I had to wonder what is my pattern? Do I have a pattern for a behavior that makes me less effective for my Lord, and how do I change the pattern so that I do not repeat the behavior? This was the topic of my conversation with God.

> **Deuteronomy 32:28-29** For they *are* a nation void of counsel, neither *is there any* understanding in them. O that they were wise, *that* they understood this, *that* they would consider their latter end!

When we fall into a pattern of bad behavior it is usually because of some lack of understanding within us that is forming our actions. We fail to see the big picture and thus sin is the natural default behavior. Sometimes a better perspective of the sin can give us the motivation to change the pattern.

Moses experienced this with the children of Israel frequently. They strayed often from trusting the Lord and they had to repeatedly learn to come back to Him. There were consequences for their behavior, but they never increased their understanding of, or dedication to the Lord to the point at which they wouldn't continually fall back into the same pattern of behavior.

Their lack of understanding (wisdom) was the root of their folly. It is the root of our folly as well. We must seek and apply wisdom so that we will understand the "latter end" of our behavior. Wisdom is the key to changing the pattern. Wisdom helps us see through the fog and see the truth, so we live righteously and don't get distracted by temptation.

In Proverbs 9, Wisdom has prepared her house and furnished her table. There is a seat for us and she is calling for all those that are looking for understanding.

Proverbs 9:5-6 Come, eat of my bread, and drink of the wine *which* I have mingled. Forsake the foolish, and live; and go in the way of understanding.

By taking Wisdom by the hand, she will lead us to understanding, freedom, and liberty. Bondage, confusion, and uncertainty exist with foolishness. Wisdom is the element that will keep us from falling back into our old pattern of behavior; old ways of doing and old ways of thinking. Wisdom leads us to truth in order to keep out of the snare that will bring us under the captivity of sin again. Wisdom will keep us from the folly of our old pattern.

Psalm 85:8 I will hear what God the LORD will speak: for he will speak peace unto his people, and to his saints: but let them not turn again to folly.

When you received Christ to be your savior you inherited more than a home in heaven. Christ made you free from the bondage of sin. This makes it possible to break the pattern of sin and live differently.

Galatians 5:1 Stand fast therefore in the liberty wherewith Christ hath made us free, and be not entangled again with the yoke of bondage.

Your salvation opens the door for you to commune with wisdom and now you have the opportunity to walk in a new way; you have access to know the truth and to change your pattern. Through Christ, you can take a hold of wisdom and be pulled out of the old pattern of behavior through obtaining greater truth and knowledge. Christ has a new pattern for you. Wisdom will give you the ability to follow it.

Face to Face With Your Lord

Have a Conversation with Your Lord Jesus

༄ Lord, what pattern of sin do I fall into?

_____
_____

༄ Lord, how have I tried to change my pattern?

_____
_____

༄ Lord, how have I tried to gain wisdom from you?

_____
_____

༄ Lord, I want a new pattern for my life. I want to change to be more like you. Please give me the wisdom to understand the error in my ways.

*Pray...*_____
_____
_____*...listen*

CONVERSATION 100

The Impossible is Possible

Related Bible Passages				
Old Testament	Psalms	Proverbs	New Testament
Deuteronomy 34	86	10	Acts 16

As you read through your Bible it is pretty easy to come to the conclusion that the characters were super-human. You read about the miraculous results of their actions and can easily believe that they had something that you don't have. That they were gifted with powers that you do not have access to. Truly, they are fantastic stories of God's amazing power working through amazing people.

While the stories in my Bible are incredible, I had to realize that they involve people that are just like you and me – flesh and blood. They struggled with family, temptation, apathy, spiritual weakness, depression and illness. They were regular people living life and trying to survive. So, what is it that makes their stories so miraculous? God's hand is what makes their stories miraculous.

> **Psalm 86:10** For thou *art* great, and doest wondrous things: thou *art* God alone.

Miraculous things are still happening, and we can have a part of the action. All we have to do is step outside of our comfort zone – for just a minute - and do something possible. Notice that I used the word "possible" and not the word "impossible." When we do what is *possible*, it creates a pathway for God to do the impossible.

In Deuteronomy, I read about the end of Moses life. His story is amazing, but when I took a closer look at what he did, I saw that it was all possible actions. He brought a mass of people through the wilderness to the doors of the promised land. He hit a rock with a stick and water came out. He raised his arms over the Red Sea and it parted. Never was Moses expected to work a miracle. He simply did what was possible and God worked the miracles and did the impossible.

In Acts chapter 16, Paul and Silas did the possible, and God did the impossible. These two men found themselves in prison because they were teaching the gospel of Christ. Paul and Silas were beaten, thrown into the inner prison and locked in stocks. Despite their horrible fate, they sang praises to God. Certainly, the jailor could hear the unexpected sounds: sounds of praise instead of screams of discontent.

Miraculously, God revealed His plan for Paul and Silas.

> **Acts 16:26** And suddenly there was a great earthquake, so that the foundations of the prison were shaken: and immediately all the doors were opened, and every one's bands were loosed.

Here is where Paul and Silas did what was possible so that God could do the impossible. Paul and Silas did not flee when the prison doors flew open. They stayed in their open cell. Through this act, the jailor was convinced that God was real and a relationship with God was available to him.

> **Acts 16:29-31** Then he called for a light, and sprang in, and came trembling, and fell down before Paul and Silas, And brought them out, and said, Sirs, what must I do to be saved? And they said, Believe on the Lord Jesus Christ, and thou shalt be saved, and thy house.

The jailor was converted that night and baptized. They left the prison with the jailor and he washed Paul and Silas' wounds and fed them. Paul and Silas returned to the prison later that night only to be released the next morning.

What did Paul and Silas do that was possible? They stayed in a bad situation in order for the Lord to fulfill His purposes.

A man and his household were saved because Paul and Silas stayed and did not flee. God was able to use their situation to work a miracle, but God did not abandon Paul and Silas after the miracle of salvation was worked. God delivered them out of their bad circumstance.

> **Proverbs 10:3** The LORD will not suffer the soul of the righteous to famish: but he casteth away the substance of the wicked.

God was not going to leave them nor forsake them in the midst of a trial, but His miracle of salvation for the jailor did require that Paul and Silas stay in an uncomfortable situation for a time.

Today, I felt God was asking me to do the possible. How about you? God may even ask for us to be physically inconvenienced for a moment to create a pathway for the impossible to happen. We might have to stay in a bad situation for a moment, we might have to experience a minute of fear, we might have to try something new, but it is all possible. When we do that thing that is possible, we might get to see that we are a part of a fantastic story when the impossible happens.

Conversations

Have a Conversation with Your Lord Jesus

🕊 Lord, have I stopped trying to do things for you because I believed I had to do the impossible?

_____
_____

🕊 Lord, is it possible that I am going through a difficult time so that you can do something amazing?

_____
_____

🕊 Lord, what can I do that is possible?

_____
_____

🕊 Lord, I know that you will never ask too much of me. I am willing to do the possible so that you can do the impossible.

*Pray...*_____

_____
...listen

Face to Face With Your Lord

CONVERSATION 101

Shine as Lights

Related Bible Passages			
Old Testament	Psalms	Proverbs	New Testament
Joshua 2	87	11	Philippians 2

Rahab was a prostitute living in Jericho. She had no connection to God and no personal knowledge of His existence. She was living a life based on a whole different set of spiritual rules and her lifestyle harmonized with those rules. From her standpoint, her lifestyle was for sustainability and may not have even been considered morally wrong; it was just a lifestyle that met her needs.

> **Proverbs 11:18** The wicked worketh a deceitful work: but to him that soweth righteousness *shall be* a sure reward.

Miraculously, Rahab did not remain in this state. Something changed her mind and she ultimately turned toward the

God of heaven. What was it that brought her to the point of turning toward God?

> **Joshua 2:9-11** And she said unto the men, I know that the LORD hath given you the land, and that your terror is fallen upon us, and that all the inhabitants of the land faint because of you. For we have heard how the LORD dried up the water of the Red sea for you, when ye came out of Egypt; and what ye did unto the two kings of the Amorites, that *were* on the other side Jordan, Sihon and Og, whom ye utterly destroyed. And as soon as we had heard *these things*, our hearts did melt, neither did there remain any more courage in any man, because of you: for the LORD your God, he *is* God in heaven above, and in earth beneath.

As I read these passages and started my conversation with my Lord, I had to consider many of my friends and neighbors that have never been introduced to the God of heaven. They have no knowledge of Him, nor do they know the name, Jesus Christ. Those that have not been introduced to the God of heaven are doing as they know how to do. They are living to sustain themselves and they may not recognize their actions as evil or wrong according to God's standards. They are simply living out the only life they know and serving their own desires. They have been raised by a different set of rules and are living a lifestyle that harmonizes with those rules.

Rahab told the men that came to her seeking protection, "...we have heard..." The power of the Lord and how He was leading and directing His people had spread, and the people of Jericho heard about what He was doing. Their hearts melted in fear, but not every heart turned in faith toward the Lord. However, through what she had heard, Rahab decided to turn her heart to believe in the Lord God. The Lord had mercy available to all men in Jericho, but only Rahab turned her fear into faith. She believed in God, and His mercy was her reward.

Rahab would not have been persuaded to trust in God if she had never heard of what He could do. It was this presentation of information that created an invitation for her to trust in God. My unbelieving friends are no different. If I want to see them converted, they must first hear of what God is doing.

As Christians, we are well aware that we are living amongst people that have no knowledge of God, but we forget that we are responsible for making the introduction. They do not know Him by name or experience. Our job is to live a life serving the Lord and speaking about His greatness amongst those that do not believe. This act could potentially cause them to take a look at Jesus Christ and consider who He is.

> **Philippians 2:14-15** Do all things without murmurings and disputings: That ye may be blameless and harmless, the sons of God, without rebuke, in the midst of a crooked and perverse nation, among whom ye shine as lights in the world;

We are to shine as a light in this world. After reading this verse, I had to consider how am I letting my light shine? How am I spreading the news of what God is doing in my life? If I am doing nothing, then I am not spreading the light and people are not being given the opportunity to hear about God.

The amazing power of God and His mercy was a shining light in Rahab's world. She came to the conclusion that, "... the LORD your God, he *is* God in heaven above, and in earth beneath." She was transformed from a heathen harlot to a believing child of God. She then became the shining light to her perverse nation. She collected her family and introduced them to the God that gave her physical and spiritual salvation.

> **Psalm 87:4** I will make mention of Rahab and Babylon to them that know me: behold Philistia, and Tyre, with Ethiopia; this *man* was born there.

Rahab is remembered for her faith, and because of her faith, this woman was brought into the lineage of Jesus Christ. God has a great love for your unbelieving friends. Even with all their sin and false beliefs, God still loves them and wants them to come to know Him. He needs you to spread the light and spread the word of what God is doing in your life. Talk of God's wondrous works, publish what He has done in your life, get the word out so people can hear and have the chance to believe.

Conversations

Have a Conversation with Your Lord Jesus

☙ Lord, how am I sharing what you are doing in my life?

_____
_____

☙ Lord, how am I sharing with my unbelieving friends what you are doing in my life?

_____
_____

☙ Lord, do I keep information about you to myself?

_____
_____

☙ Lord, I want people to hear about you and understand how amazing you are. I want them to know that a relationship with you is possible.

*Pray...*_____
_____
_____*...listen*

Face to Face with Your Lord

ABOUT THE AUTHOR

Danika Salmans lives in Wyoming with her husband and three children. She has been serving as a pastor's wife for many years. Her prayer is that this series will be used to spark a deeper, more vibrant relationship with the Lord Jesus through Bible reading and real conversations with Him. Her hope and prayer are that you will use her conversations in this volume as a foundation to spark your own, Face to Face conversation with your Lord.

May the conversations continue...

Face to Face With Your Lord

Use the following pages to journal your own conversations with your Lord Jesus.

My Conversations

FACE TO FACE WITH MY LORD

If you would like more opportunity to write and preserve these precious conversations with your Lord, a full-length journal will soon be available from Amazon.

CONVERSATION DATE _____

BIBLE READING

Old Testament	Psalms	Proverbs	New Testament

Lord, when I consider my day and what I am experiencing in my life, what passages have given me some clarity and understanding?

_____

_____

_____

_____

_____

_____

_____

_____

Conversations

Lord, when I consider my spiritual condition, what are you encouraging me to do differently?

_____
_____
_____
_____
_____
_____
_____
_____
_____
_____
_____
_____

Lord, what passage have you given me today that will give me some encouragement and direction?

_____
_____
_____
_____
_____
_____
_____
_____
_____
_____
_____
_____

Face to Face With Your Lord

NOTES: Verses to ponder and discuss with my Lord throughout the day...

Conversations

Face to Face with Your Lord

CONVERSATION DATE _____

BIBLE READING

Old Testament	Psalms	Proverbs	New Testament

Lord, when I consider my day and what I am experiencing in my life, what passages have given me some clarity and understanding?

_____
_____
_____
_____
_____
_____
_____
_____
_____
_____

Conversations

Lord, when I consider my spiritual condition, what are you encouraging me to do differently?

_____
_____
_____
_____
_____
_____
_____
_____
_____
_____
_____
_____

Lord, what passage have you given me today that will give me some encouragement and direction?

_____
_____
_____
_____
_____
_____
_____
_____
_____
_____
_____
_____

NOTES: Verses to ponder and discuss with my Lord throughout the day...

Conversations

CONVERSATION DATE _____

BIBLE READING

Old Testament	Psalms	Proverbs	New Testament

Lord, when I consider my day and what I am experiencing in my life, what passages have given me some clarity and understanding?

_____
_____
_____
_____
_____
_____
_____
_____

Conversations

Lord, when I consider my spiritual condition, what are you encouraging me to do differently?

_____
_____
_____
_____
_____
_____
_____
_____
_____
_____
_____

Lord, what passage have you given me today that will give me some encouragement and direction?

_____
_____
_____
_____
_____
_____
_____
_____
_____
_____
_____

NOTES: Verses to ponder and discuss with my Lord throughout the day...

Conversations

Face to Face with Your Lord

CONVERSATION DATE _____

BIBLE READING

Old Testament	Psalms	Proverbs	New Testament

Lord, when I consider my day and what I am experiencing in my life, what passages have given me some clarity and understanding?

_____
_____
_____
_____
_____
_____
_____
_____

Conversations

Lord, when I consider my spiritual condition, what are you encouraging me to do differently?

_____
_____
_____
_____
_____
_____
_____
_____
_____
_____
_____

Lord, what passage have you given me today that will give me some encouragement and direction?

_____
_____
_____
_____
_____
_____
_____
_____
_____
_____
_____

NOTES: Verses to ponder and discuss with my Lord throughout the day...

Connect with others on Social Media

What did the Lord show you today? Has the Lord shown you something special? Do you need encouragement, or can you offer encouragement to someone else? Connect with others that are having conversations with the Lord.

FACEBOOK:
Conversations: Face to Face With Your Lord
@GloryStrengthBeauty

TWITTER:
@danika_salmans

INSTAGRAM:
danika_salmans
#Face2Face

WEBSITE:
GloryStrengthAndBeauty.com

Face to Face With Your Lord

Face to Face with Your Lord

The Conversation Continues

These titles are all available from Amazon. More books are to come.

Book 1 – Conversations: Face to Face with Your Lord
Conversations 1- 58
$12.95

Book 2 – Conversations: Face to Face with Your Lord
Conversations 59-101
$12.95

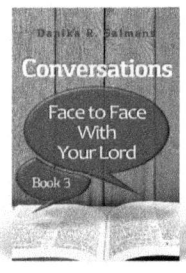

Book 3 – Conversations: Face to Face with Your Lord
Conversations 102-144
$12.95

www.ingramcontent.com/pod-product-compliance
Lightning Source LLC
Chambersburg PA
CBHW070847050426
42453CB00012B/2082